I0025516

Beyond Growth

TOWARDS A NEW ECONOMIC APPROACH

OECD

This work is published under the responsibility of the Secretary-General of the OECD. The opinions expressed and arguments employed herein do not necessarily reflect the official views of OECD member countries.

This document, as well as any data and map included herein, are without prejudice to the status of or sovereignty over any territory, to the delimitation of international frontiers and boundaries and to the name of any territory, city or area.

The statistical data for Israel are supplied by and under the responsibility of the relevant Israeli authorities. The use of such data by the OECD is without prejudice to the status of the Golan Heights, East Jerusalem and Israeli settlements in the West Bank under the terms of international law.

Note by Turkey
The information in this document with reference to "Cyprus" relates to the southern part of the Island. There is no single authority representing both Turkish and Greek Cypriot people on the Island. Turkey recognises the Turkish Republic of Northern Cyprus (TRNC). Until a lasting and equitable solution is found within the context of the United Nations, Turkey shall preserve its position concerning the "Cyprus issue".

Note by all the European Union Member States of the OECD and the European Union
The Republic of Cyprus is recognised by all members of the United Nations with the exception of Turkey. The information in this document relates to the area under the effective control of the Government of the Republic of Cyprus.

Please cite this publication as:
OECD (2020), *Beyond Growth: Towards a New Economic Approach*, New Approaches to Economic Challenges, OECD Publishing, Paris, *https://doi.org/10.1787/33a25ba3-en*.

ISBN 978-92-64-79898-4 (print)
ISBN 978-92-64-63834-1 (pdf)

New Approaches to Economic Challenges
ISSN 2707-7926 (print)
ISSN 2707-7934 (online)

Preface

This report was produced by an Advisory Group on a New Growth Narrative that we brought together on behalf of the Secretary-General of the OECD in 2018. Experts drawn from a diverse range of fields with whom we have worked in different instances, the members of the group brought together various threads of new thinking on economics in order to weave a new narrative on economic growth.

Prior to the Global Financial Crisis, there were already cogent critiques on dominant economic analyses. This intensified sharply in the wake of the crisis and the protracted recovery that followed. It became increasingly clear that conventional economic theories and policies had been found wanting. Many OECD economies were, to varying degrees, beset by rising inequalities, slower productivity growth, increasing corporate concentration, a ratcheting-up of debt levels, environmental degradation (notably via climate change) and financial instability. These issues connected to a prevailing narrative based on the primacy of growth and stressed market liberalisation and deregulation together with fiscal discipline and low tax rates and curbing social welfare benefits. That narrative not only abetted the failure to address acute social and environmental challenges, but also failed on its own terms: the growth of productivity and per capita incomes has been increasingly anaemic in recent decades.

This report points to a new narrative, one based on a broader conception of economic progress, richer frameworks for economic, social and environmental analysis and a wider set of policy objectives. It confirms the need for a people-centred narrative, which the OECD has been proposing for some years now.

As regards the objectives of economic policy, it urges a move away from the traditional emphasis on GDP growth to a multi-dimensional conception of economic progress comprising environmental sustainability, rising human well-being, falling inequality and system resilience. The prioritisation of efficiency objectives may have undermined the resilience of societies by overlooking equity and sustainability objectives. The emergence of the Covid-19 pandemic exacerbated previous trends, with clear asymmetric impacts among different income groups. Embracing a multi-dimensional set of objectives, as advocated by this report, and promoted by the OECD, would enable assessment of trade-offs, and complementarities, as well as identification of unintended consequences, to better guide policy choices and decision making.

In terms of how we think about economies, it calls for moving away from simplistic assumptions such as homogeneous, rational, utility-maximising agents interacting in timeless self-equilibrating markets. It instead suggests further engagement and experimentation with complexity, path-dependence, bounded rationality, economic power, multiple equilibria and non-equilibrium outcomes. It encourages us to see modern economies as complex adaptive systems, constantly evolving and reorganising rather than a series of deviations from a stable equilibrium with the ability to self-stabilise when hit by shocks.

I personally support these key messages. What is more, during my time at the OECD, we took the lead in putting these ideas into practice through three major initiatives: New Approaches to Economic Challenges (NAEC), the Better Life, and Inclusive Growth Initiatives. The Organisation has made progress in advancing a new approach like the one proposed in this report, one organised around well-being and reflecting the goals of environmental sustainability, social equality and system resilience. Such an approach requires an understanding of how the economy works, and breaking out of the silos that contributed to the perilous situation in which we find ourselves today.

The report was largely written before the Covid-19 outbreak, but its key lessons are sharpened and amplified by the pandemic and the economic and social crisis it precipitated. This systemic crisis, like the previous one, has revealed key fragilities in our economies and societies. On the health front, major vulnerabilities were exposed, reflecting both market failures (e.g. weak incentives to discover and produce vaccines) and government failures (e.g. underfunded health systems in many countries, lack of universal access to health care in some and gaps in social protection systems). "Just in time" production systems compounded these vulnerabilities. In many places, public investment and social safety nets had been eroded by years of fiscal austerity after the last crisis, and in some countries, there had already long been a dominant ethos of curbing the size of government and cutting taxes.

The new growth narrative heralded in this report is useful not only to understand this latest crisis, but also to think about how to emerge from it and "build back better". We must avoid the mistakes of the past. In particular, we have to do a better job of confronting a series of converging planetary emergencies linked to the environment, the economy, and our social and political systems. We have to operationalise the insights coming out of NAEC about feedback loops between different systems and the consequent need to enhance resilience. In order to deal with future shocks, whether another financial crisis, the climate emergency, or societal fragmentation, our analysis should rely on solid, integrated analytical frameworks based on multi-disciplinarity.

The current crisis, while calamitous in many respects, may provoke a much-needed wholesale rethink. The crisis has demonstrated that business-as-usual approaches can be disrupted, even radically, when there is a necessity to do so. It has starkly illustrated the interaction of complex systems and the possibility of cascading failures. It has provided a reminder of the benefits of resilience, for example via the maintenance of spare capacity and margins for error, and underlined the vital importance of public services, particularly health and social care. Not least, it has provided examples of solidarity, public spirit, self-sacrifice and a renewed requirement for multilateralism to solve global problems. While the road out of the current crisis is bound to be long and difficult, the prospects for achieving a new narrative is a source of hope.

There is still a long way to go, however, both within the OECD and beyond. Notably, there is further need to develop and apply models that can better reflect reality emphasised in this report, that modern economies are emergent complex systems, indeed part of a "system of systems", which are not well characterised by the concept of equilibrium. This might help us better balance just-in-time considerations with just-in-case ones, something the current crisis suggests is necessary. Achieving this shift will not be easy: the task is beset by difficulties of both a technical and political economy nature. Abandoning the many simplifying assumptions made in standard economic theory can quickly make models intractable and/or hard to explain. And the simple fact is that those with economic and political power have a vested interest in preserving the approaches that have served them, though not most others, well.

The members of the Advisory Group, highly respected experts from outside the Organisation, have contributed their proposals on what needs to change in economics, analysis and policymaking. They have succeeded admirably, and I would like to thank them for being so generous in accepting Secretary General Gurría's invitation, and so inspiring in the insights they have offered. In particular, I would like to thank Michael Jacobs for taking the lead in producing this report, skilfully weaving together the rich and varied ideas coming from the whole group and contributing his own expertise and proposals. My appreciation goes also to William Hynes and the NAEC team at the OECD, for their efforts and strong commitment to advance this transformative agenda.

Gabriela Ramos
Assistant Director-General for Social and Human Sciences
UNESCO

Foreword

Launched in May 2015, OECD Secretary-General Angel Gurría's '21 for 21' proposal called for the consolidation and further transformation of the OECD, including by 'redefining the growth narrative to put the well-being of people at the centre of our efforts.'

To contribute to this debate, in 2018 the Secretary-General commissioned an Advisory Group on a New Growth Narrative to examine how economic, social and environmental considerations could be integrated in a coherent approach. Acting in a personal capacity, the Advisory Group comprises Andy Haldane, Michael Jacobs, Alan Kirman, Nora Lustig, Mariana Mazzucato, Robert Skidelsky, Dennis Snower and Roberto Unger.[1] Members of the Advisory Group serve in a personal capacity. They endorse the broad arguments made in this report but should not necessarily be taken as agreeing with every word. The Group has sought to bring together in a single, short and readable document various strands of new economic thinking curated over recent years by the New Approaches to Economic Challenges (NAEC) initiative. *Beyond Growth: Towards a New Economic Approach* is their report.

The report has been written and coordinated by Michael Jacobs, with research assistance by Merve Sancak at the Sheffield Political Economy Research Institute. The project has been overseen by Gabriela Ramos, former Chief of Staff and Sherpa, with the support of William Hynes, the NAEC Co-ordinator.

The report attempts to synthesise a wide range of reflection on new ways of thinking about economic policymaking. It encompasses a new set of goals and measures of economic and social progress; new frameworks of economic analysis; and new approaches to policy.

While reactions from OECD members are strongly welcomed, this is not an OECD report requiring approval. Nor is it exhaustive in the content covered. Focusing on the challenges facing OECD countries, it builds on the NAEC reports *New Approaches to Economic Challenges: Towards a New Narrative*, presented at OECD Week in 2017, and *Elements of a New Growth Narrative* (SG/NAEC(2018)1), discussed at the NAEC Group meeting in September 2018 marking 10 years since the collapse of Lehman Brothers.

The opinions expressed and the arguments employed herein do not necessarily reflect the official views of OECD member countries, nor any institution with which the contributors may be affiliated.

Note

[1] Andy Haldane is Chief Economist of the Bank of England.
Michael Jacobs is Professorial Fellow in the Sheffield Political Economy Research Institute at the University of Sheffield.
Alan Kirman is Professor Emeritus of Economics at the Aix-Marseille University and at the Ecole des Hautes Etudes en Sciences Sociales, and senior adviser to NAEC.
Nora Lustig is the Samuel Z. Stone Professor of Latin American Economics in the Department of Economics at Tulane University.
Mariana Mazzucato is Professor in the Economics of Innovation and Public Value at University College London (UCL), and Founding Director of the UCL Institute for Innovation and Public Purpose.
Robert Skidelsky is Emeritus Professor of Political Economy at the University of Warwick.
Dennis Snower is founder and President of the Global Solutions Initiative and the Global Economic Symposium and was President of the Kiel Institute for the World Economy and Professor of Economics at the Christian-Albrechts-University of Kiel until February 2019. He is a Senior Research Fellow at the Blavatnik School of Government, University of Oxford.
Roberto Mangabeira Unger is Roscoe Pound Professor of Law at Harvard University.

Table of contents

Follow OECD Publications on:

http://twitter.com/OECD_Pubs

http://www.facebook.com/OECDPublications

http://www.linkedin.com/groups/OECD-Publications-4645871

http://www.youtube.com/oecdilibrary

OECD Alerts http://www.oecd.org/oecddirect/

Executive Summary

The need for a new economic approach

The Covid-19 crisis requires our societies to make critical choices about the kind of economies we wish to rebuild. Coming on top of the financial crisis, and the climate change and heightened inequalities widely experienced in the last decade, the global pandemic has raised serious questions about the nature of our economic system.

The world faces profound economic, environmental and social challenges, but many of the policies implemented over the last forty years or so are no longer able to improve economic and social outcomes in the ways they once promised. Four trends are combining to make the need for change pressing.

Accelerating environmental crisis is the most urgent. To keep the average surface temperature rise to 1.5C, global greenhouse gas emissions must be approximately halved by 2030, and reach net zero by around 2050. That is a transformative task of unprecedented proportions, made greater by the need to tackle simultaneously biodiversity loss, soil degradation, and pollution.

Rapid technological change is transforming many aspects of our economies, changing the numbers and kinds of jobs and the ways they are organised. Multinational companies, including digital platforms, have grown to positions of market dominance unrivalled in the modern era.

New patterns of globalisation are also emerging. Investment and trade continue to shift to the south and east of the world, as large transnational corporations form complex global production networks and supply chains.

Demographic change underpins each of these trends, with ageing societies calling into question the ability of those of working age to support non-working age populations. Intergenerational inequalities are compounding inequalities of income, wealth, gender and race.

Elements of a new economic narrative

Addressing these challenges requires rethinking many of the dominant approaches to economic policymaking which OECD countries have adopted over the last 40 years. This will involve:

- A new conception of economic and social progress – a deeper understanding of the relationship between growth, human wellbeing, a reduction in inequalities and environmental sustainability, which can inform economic policymaking and politics.
- New frameworks of economic theory and analysis – a richer basis of understanding and evidence on how economies work, and new tools and techniques to help policymakers devise policy.
- New approaches to economic policy – a wider set of policy and institutional reforms, based on the new frameworks and analysis, to achieve the new social and economic goals.

Four objectives for economic policymaking should be paramount within this framework:

- Environmental sustainability – understood as a path of rapidly declining greenhouse gas emissions and environmental degradation, consistent with avoiding catastrophic damage and achieving a stable and healthy level of ecosystem services.

- Rising wellbeing – understood as an improving level of life satisfaction for individuals, and a rising sense of improvement in the quality of life and condition of society as a whole.

- Falling inequality – understood as a reduction in the gap between the incomes and wealth of the richest and poorest groups in society, a reduction in rates of poverty, and a relative improvement in the wellbeing, incomes and opportunities of those experiencing systematic disadvantage, including women, members of ethnic minorities, disabled people, and those in disadvantaged geographic communities.

- System resilience – understood as the economy's ability to withstand financial, environmental or other shocks without catastrophic and system-wide effects.

Countries which seek to achieve these four goals, rather than giving overwhelming priority to growth, will experience a more balanced path of economic and social development, which will better serve both people and planet.

Over recent years, much of the framework of orthodox economic theory which previously underpinned much policymaking has been challenged and superseded. Across a range of fields, and arising from both mainstream and 'heterodox' traditions, modern economics has developed new forms of economic analysis. These should now inform economic policymaking by governments and international institutions.

The deep challenges facing OECD economies today will not be addressed simply by incremental changes to existing policies. Reforms to achieve the new goals need to be built in to the core structures and dynamics of economies. This will require a more profound shift, of the kind which occurred in previous eras of crisis and change, in the 1940s and 1980s. But many such policy proposals have been made, and there is a wealth of insight and understanding which now exists across the field of academic economics and economic policy making, from which solutions can be drawn.

Beyond Growth: Towards a New Economic Approach

This report explains why a new approach to economic analysis and policy is needed. It sets out the multiple challenges now facing almost all economies and proposes a new set of overarching policy goals: environmental sustainability, a reduction in inequalities, improved wellbeing, and system resilience. Achieving these goals requires policymakers to look 'beyond growth'. The report argues that the dominant approach to economic policymaking over the last forty years, based on an orthodox and subsequently revised model of neoclassical economic theory, is not adequate to address these challenges. It describes the various analytical advances which have been made in economics in recent decades which offer a richer understanding of how economies work. It argues that overcoming these challenges requires structural rather than incremental reform, and sets out a range of policy approaches, drawn from the new analytical frameworks, which might help achieve these wider economic and social goals.

Introduction: Why we need a new economic approach

The Covid-19 crisis which has engulfed the world in 2020 has caused human suffering and economic disruption on an unprecedented scale. As countries face the daunting task of economic recovery while still managing the public health risks of the pandemic, few people are predicting a return to 'normal'. It seems inevitable that our economies and societies 'after Covid' will be different from the ones that found themselves overwhelmed as the virus struck.

This is a moment, therefore, of profound choice. It is one in which we cannot avoid asking what kind of future we should be seeking to create out of the crisis.

The many calls now heard to 'build back better' arise partly from problems which the crisis has itself exposed. Despite clear and recent warnings from scientists and public health officials, few countries were ready for a pandemic of this kind.[1] At the same time our economies have proved less resilient than we had assumed. Many countries' health and social care systems have not been able to cope. Reliance on globalised supply chains based on 'just-in-time' efficiencies has been called into question.[2] Almost everywhere the crisis has revealed the impact of inequality: so far from being a 'great leveller', Covid-19 and its economic consequences have hit the poor and vulnerable the hardest.[3].

At the same time, the crisis has also created new opportunities. The re-emergence of clean air in many cities round the world has saved many lives even as others were lost.[4] Nature has found new places in which to flourish. The enforced reduction in consumption and commuting has led many people to question what kind of lifestyle best contributes to wellbeing. Perhaps most of all, governments have found that in a crisis they can intervene in their economies at huge scale and speed. The macroeconomic arguments over government spending and debt are of course not over, but the consensus that a crisis of this magnitude justifies such intervention – and with the assistance of central banks can be paid for over the long term - has been notable.[5]

The debate on these and other lessons of the crisis that has occurred over recent months has been important. But it has perhaps not yet been profound enough. For it is not just one crisis that our societies face. What is striking about the last decade is that developed economies in particular have effectively been experiencing a running series of crises. The long aftermath of the financial crash of 2008 is still not over, with stagnant productivity and continued financial risk among the most obvious overhanging problems. The financial crisis is widely held to have exacerbated inequalities which in turn have contributed in many countries to political conflict and instability. And throughout the last decade there has been a gathering crisis of climate change and wider environmental breakdown, which threatens to become overwhelming over the coming decades if not radically addressed. And now we have had a global pandemic and its consequent public health crisis and economic depression.

The confluence of such crises should surely make governments and publics sit up. It would be surprising if it were just coincidence that so many deep problems have occurred at the same time. At the very least they surely demand that we seek to understand not just their individual causes but their inter-relationships. And in doing so that we examine the nature of the economic system and economic policies from which they have arisen – or at least which have not prevented them. This is what this report seeks to do.

To do this it is vital that we start from an understanding of the nature of challenges which, even before the Covid-19 crisis, our economies were experiencing – and which, after it, we will therefore continue to face. For without this we shall not be able to address the question of what building a better post-Covid economy and society will require.

Of these challenges, accelerating environmental crisis is without doubt the most urgent. The 2018 report of the Intergovernmental Panel on Climate Change made clear that, to achieve the international goal of holding the average surface temperature rise to 1.5 degrees Celsius, global emissions of greenhouse gases must be approximately halved by 2030, and reach net zero by around the middle of the century.[6] That is a transformative task of unprecedented proportions. It is made even greater by the need to tackle simultaneously a series of other worsening – and inter-related – global environmental problems, including biodiversity loss, soil degradation, and air and marine pollution, as documented in the 2019 reports of the UN Environment Programme and the Intergovernmental Science-Policy Platform on Biodiversity and Ecosystem Services.[7].

At the same time, rapid technological change has been transforming many aspects of our economies. There is much to celebrate in the processes of innovation, from new consumer goods to new ways of doing business. But there are significant challenges too. The development of automation technologies, particularly artificial intelligence, is changing both the numbers and kinds of jobs our economies generate and the ways they are organized, leading to widespread concerns about the 'future of work'.[8] In a variety of sectors, major multinational companies, including digital platforms, have grown to positions of market dominance unrivalled in the modern era, raising questions about both their economic and social impact and the implications for public policy.[9] In many countries there is increasing debate about the impact of new technologies on issues ranging from democracy to mental health.[10].

New patterns of globalisation are also emerging. Investment and trade continue to shift to the south and east of the world, as large transnational corporations form complex global production networks and supply chains.[11] The 'financialisation' of most advanced economies has continued, with higher levels of private debt than in the past, higher returns to holders of financial assets, and in some cases larger financial sectors relative to the rest of the economy.[12] National financial regulation is made harder by the combination of a globalised financial system and new financial technologies.[13]

Underpinning each of these trends is demographic change. Many developed societies are significantly ageing, raising questions about the ability of those of working age to support non-working age populations, and all are experiencing the pressures as well as the benefits of increased migration.[14] Many developing countries are simultaneously experiencing rapid population growth.

These challenges would be considerable in any circumstances. But they come after a period in which most OECD economies have performed substantially less well than in the past. The 2008 financial crisis exposed serious flaws not just in financial regulation but in the credit-based form of growth which preceded it. Its effects continue to play out. For most countries, the recovery after the 2008-9 recession was among the slowest on record. Before the Covid-19 crisis economic growth had been restored, but it was generally fragile, still dependent on the emergency life-support of ultra-low interest rates and hugely expanded central bank balance sheets.[15] Public and private debt levels as a proportion of national income were still high in many countries even before their recent surge.[16] Productivity growth had stalled in some countries, and was historically low in many others; innovation at the technological frontier was no longer being diffused to the rest of the economy as it had been in the past.[17].

Inequalities have risen in most advanced countries over recent decades, particularly between the incomes of the top 1% of the population and those of the rest of society. Wealth inequality, in particular, has grown, in large part due to the appreciation in the value of assets, itself a cause of financial volatility.[18] In many countries, unemployment had remained stubbornly high even before the present recession, particularly for young people.[19] Most developed economies have seen an increase in under-employment and insecure and precarious work of different kinds, from self-employment and part-time work to very short term contracts.[20] In some countries average earnings had stagnated, with living standards for many households barely above those of a decade ago, or maintained only via rising household debt.[21] In many the gap between richer regions and those on the periphery has widened.[22]

Not all OECD countries have experienced all of these problems. Some have done better than others. But many have experienced the political consequences which have followed from a decade of economic under-performance and accompanying global pressures, alongside other more directly political causes. Popular discontent with politicians and the political system has been rising over a long period in many countries.[23]

Trust in established institutions, in experts and 'elites' has declined.[24] Societies which once experienced high levels of social cohesion are now widely felt to be more fragmented, prone to cultural as well as economic divisions.[25] In many countries large numbers of people report feelings of economic and political disempowerment – a sense that society has become less fair, with a widening gap between the lives of the richest and the majority, and that in a more globalised world national societies have somehow 'lost control' of their own destinies.[26] Perhaps as a consequence, political parties which once dominated government have seen their vote shares fall, in some cases dramatically, with 'populist' parties of various kinds gaining ground, and some entering government.[27] In many countries (though not all) there is a widespread sense of social and economic conflict and crisis.

In these circumstances it is not surprising that, even before the Covid-19 crisis, politicians and commentators from across the political spectrum – not to mention many voters – were questioning whether current and conventional economic policies were sufficient to address the challenges and problems their countries face. Many of the policies which have been implemented across the OECD, not just over the last decade but over the last forty years or so, appeared no longer able to improve economic and social outcomes in the ways they once promised. For example, in an era in which low interest rates and low growth rates seem entrenched – the phenomenon sometimes described as 'secular stagnation'[28] – it had become clear that monetary policy alone is insufficient to manage the macro-economy. Reliance upon it leaves policymakers with particularly few levers to deal with recession.[29] As a knowledge-based economy becomes more digitalised, with 'intangible' investment increasingly important and a growing divide between firms at the cutting edge of innovation and those falling behind, new approaches will be needed to raise productivity across the economy as a whole, and ensure this reduces inequalities rather than exacerbates them.[30] Normal labour market policies have not been able to sustain demand for lower-skilled jobs in the face of automation and globalisation, or counter the growing divide between those in secure jobs and those in precarious ones. Redistributive welfare policies have seen their effectiveness reduced, and are not sufficient to counter rising inequalities; environmental policy has failed to prevent catastrophic risk. Competition policy has not kept pace with the growth of near-monopoly companies with operations across national borders. New approaches will be required if systemic risk is to be eliminated from the financial system.[31].

Of course, OECD countries have not all followed exactly the same path in this period. Economic policies have differed, not least under different kinds of governments. But it is also true that there has been a widespread consensus on the broad contours of what makes for a successful economy.[32] It has been widely accepted, for example, that increasing global trade is a goal in itself, with countries doing better the more integrated they are into international trade and capital flows. Most countries have sought to make their financial and labour markets more 'efficient', deregulating and liberalising them where possible to widen the opportunities for financial activity and reduce restrictions on businesses. Central bank independence to conduct monetary policy has been accompanied by constraints on public borrowing. Corporation taxes have been reduced almost everywhere, and in many cases marginal personal income tax rates too. Economic growth has continued to be the dominant goal of economic policy, from which it is assumed other objectives will flow. Material consumption has been taken as a proxy for progress and development. Equity and environmental considerations have largely been dealt with 'after the event' rather than as integral to economic policy.

In the period before the financial crisis, this economic model (often described as the 'Washington Consensus') was strongly influenced by a particular form of economic analysis. Based on an orthodox version of 'neoclassical' economic theory, this assumed that the liberalisation of markets would generally improve their efficiency in allocating resources, and would therefore tend to optimise overall economic welfare. Although markets sometimes failed – for example in the presence of negative externalities, or in the provision of public goods – governments were also seen as prone to failure. They tended to have less information than market actors, and to be captured vested interests. So policy rooted in this kind of analysis tended to be sceptical of government intervention, with deregulation of various kinds widely favoured.

Over the last decade (and in some fields for longer) policy makers have modified some aspects of this analytical framework. Drawing on longstanding developments in academic economics, it has been acknowledged that orthodox neoclassical analysis has limitations: that liberalised markets are not always efficient and market failures can be significant.[33] Policy makers have recognised the need for greater government intervention, in fields such as labour market, regional and environmental policy, as well as in monetary and financial policy. In many of these fields, and others, the OECD has supported these new analytical and policy developments.

These shifts have been important. But in the face of the profound challenges and problems our economies now face, we do not believe they have yet gone far enough. For within the fields of economics and political economy, the last few decades have seen the flowering of other, more profound forms of rethinking. A variety of economic theories, evidence and techniques have been developed which offer richer ways of understanding how economies work, and how they can be made to work better. Analytical methods and models based on the new powers of data collection and computing, for example, have opened up insights not available to previous generations. Taken together, a 21st century economics has begun to come into view which looks more able to help policymakers find solutions to the 21st century economic problems they now confront.

Since 2012 the OECD's New Approaches to Economic Challenges initiative has attempted to bring together much of this new thinking, and many parts of the OECD and member states have engaged strongly with it.[34] It has benefited from the ideas of a range of researchers and institutions around the world. The debates have been deep and much has been learned.[35] It is now possible to see how many of these critiques and explorations can be brought together to create a 'new economic narrative'. Broadly speaking, this consists of three elements:

- A new conception of economic and social progress – a deeper understanding of the relationship between growth, human wellbeing, a reduction in inequalities and environmental sustainability, which can inform economic policymaking and politics.
- New frameworks of economic theory and analysis – a richer basis of understanding and evidence on how economies work, and new tools and techniques to help policymakers devise policy.
- New approaches to economic policy – a wider set of policy and institutional reforms, based on the new frameworks and analysis, to achieve the new social and economic goals.

This report aims to explain these elements and how they fit together. It was written largely before the Covid-19 crisis hit. But we believe in the face of the current crisis it is even more relevant.

At the core of the report is a recognition of the sociality of human beings and their embeddedness in social institutions, an idea with profound implications for our understanding of both economic theory and policy. We do not claim that there is a new fully-developed model of economic policy which can simply replace those which have been dominant over the last forty years. On the contrary, we do not believe that any simple model can be applied in countries with different economies, institutions and cultures. But we do believe that a new approach is needed. In setting this out we hope to stimulate debate on how, by drawing more effectively on these new developments in economics, decision makers and policy makers can make better sense of the economies we live in today, and can be provided with more effective tools to achieve their goals. This moment surely demands it

Economic and social progress and the goals of economic policy

For over seventy years, economic growth has been the dominant goal of economic policy, and the principal measure of an economy's success. And with good reason: for much of this period, rising national income signified rising household incomes, and with them average living standards. Economic growth raised employment levels, reduced poverty rates, and provided the tax receipts to finance higher government spending on public services. In most OECD countries, up to the 1980s, economic growth was accompanied by falling inequality[36] and – as higher gross domestic product (GDP) allowed more resources to go into air and water pollution control – better local environmental quality.[37] So while governments always had a wider set of economic objectives than simply rising GDP, economic growth was a pretty good metric for overall economic performance.

It would be much harder to make this claim today. Economic growth continues to generate the benefits of higher national income. But at the same time, the dominant patterns of growth in OECD countries over recent decades have also generated significant harms.

First, GDP growth is now widely associated with rising inequalities. In almost all OECD countries, the last forty years have seen a declining share of national income going to wages and salaries (labour), with a rising share going to the owners of capital.[38] With capital ownership increasingly concentrated among those on the highest incomes, the result has been a growth of both income and wealth inequality, particularly between the top 1% and 10% and the rest of the population.[39] In some countries aggregate GDP growth over the last two decades has been particularly skewed towards those on higher incomes, leaving average earnings only slowly rising, and in some cases more or less stagnant. In the US this has been going on for much longer.[40] In such circumstances GDP growth no longer translates into rising living standards for those on median and lower incomes. In some countries high rates of poverty remain a persistent blight.[41]

Second, GDP growth is no longer correlated with improvements in wellbeing. The study of wellbeing has advanced greatly in recent decades. Income is important, particularly for those whose incomes are low. But we now understand that people's sense of a fulfilled and flourishing life comes also from a wide variety of other factors: from the security and satisfaction they experience in work; their physical and mental health, social networks and personal and family relationships; and from social goods such as the levels of crime and trust in society, and the quality of public services such as health and education.[42] None of these are automatically improved simply by higher GDP, and can often be harmed by the ways it is generated - particularly for those on lower incomes and in more precarious work, and where private consumption is prioritised over public goods. For most people today, rising GDP is no longer a sufficient measure either of their own wellbeing or their sense of society's economic progress.[43]

Third, severe environmental degradation has forced a recognition that today's patterns of economic growth are undermining our capacity to maintain current standards of living. An economic system based on fossil fuels, present forms of intensive and meat-based agriculture and the unlimited exploitation of global natural resources is not sustainable over the long term. Climate change, air and marine pollution and ecological breakdown are already damaging the lives and livelihoods of millions of people around the world; they risk catastrophic damage to our economies and societies within the next few decades unless currently dominant forms of production and consumption are radically changed.[44]

These developments do not mean that economic growth should be abandoned as a goal of economic policy. Rather, they force attention to the *form* of economic growth which a country experiences and aims to achieve. It is not enough for GDP to be rising, if the underlying patterns of growth are generating significant harms at the same time. It is the *type* of economic activity which matters.

This is why we believe politicians and policymakers need to go 'beyond growth'. They need to ensure that, alongside rising GDP – and as a result of it – economic policy is achieving a wider set of objectives and measures of economic and social progress. We can no longer rely on economic growth on its own to make our societies better off.

In our view, four objectives for economic policy making should today be paramount:

- Environmental sustainability – understood as a path of rapidly declining greenhouse gas emissions and environmental degradation, consistent with avoiding catastrophic damage and achieving a stable and healthy level of ecosystem services.

- Rising wellbeing – understood as an improving level of life satisfaction for individuals, and a rising sense of improvement in the quality of life and condition of society as a whole.

- Falling inequality – understood as a reduction in the gap between the incomes and wealth of the richest and poorest groups in society, a reduction in rates of poverty, and a relative improvement in the wellbeing, incomes and opportunities of those experiencing systematic disadvantage, including women, members of ethnic minorities, disabled people, and those in disadvantaged geographic communities.

- System resilience – understood as the economy's ability to withstand financial, environmental or other shocks without catastrophic and system-wide effects.

Countries which seek to achieve these four goals, rather than giving overwhelming priority to growth, will experience a more balanced path of economic and social development, with better outcomes for both current and future generations. If we were to suggest a simple phrase to summarise this, we might describe it as a path of development which meets the needs of both people and planet.

It used to be widely thought that policy makers could not achieve such goals simultaneously. Inequality was the inevitable price of growth; environmental sustainability and growth worked essentially against one another; green policies were likely to hurt the poor. It is certainly true that such trade-offs exist in some circumstances. But it is also – and much more interestingly – true that in others these goals can be achieved together. Indeed the evidence suggests that there can be strong synergies between them.

In particular, the rising weight of international evidence in recent years has shown that – contrary to the view once widely held – reducing economic inequalities can benefit rather than harm growth.[45] There are multiple reasons for this. Most obviously, inequalities of income and opportunity prevent some people from achieving their full economic potential. Low educational attainment and skills, discrimination in the labour market, and the difficulties of working in the absence of adequate child and social care, all tend to constrain the productive resources of the economy.[46] As the OECD's work on the 'productivity-inclusiveness nexus' has shown, addressing slow productivity growth in lagging firms and regions will drive both growth and reduced inequality.[47] At the same time, people on low incomes tend to spend a higher proportion of their income than the wealthy, who are more likely to save. So improving the earnings of poorer people has a much larger impact on consumption and aggregate demand, and therefore growth, than raising the income and wealth of the relatively well off.[48]

It is also now clear that inequality tends to make economies more unstable, as the higher savings of the rich are channelled into financial and real estate assets prone to volatility. More unequal economies tend statistically to have shorter periods of growth.[49] And politically, rising inequality has tended to result in policies skewed towards the wealthy, including (for example) pressures to reduce tax rates. These in turn tend to reduce spending on the public goods, such as education, health and childcare, which can improve the economy's productive potential.[50]

The empirical evidence does not show that unequal societies are poorer than more equal ones. There are rich countries with high levels of inequality, and others which are more egalitarian. But it does show that more unequal economies do less well than they would if they were more equal.[51] In this sense it can be said that fairness and prosperity go hand in hand.

If reducing inequality can boost growth, it also has an important impact on both social and individual wellbeing. Studies across developed countries show strong correlations between inequality and a variety of other social harms, including higher rates of mental and physical ill-health, obesity and crime, and lower levels of social trust, educational attainment and social mobility.[52] This is true not just for those on low incomes, but across the population as a whole. Surveys of wellbeing consistently show that more equal societies are also those where life satisfaction and happiness are highest.[53]

The trade-offs between economic growth and environment sustainability are deeper. But by changing what is produced in the economy and how, it is now clearly possible to reduce environmental damage very significantly even while output increases.[54] Rapidly cutting greenhouse gas emissions, for example, will require significant investments in energy efficiency, renewable energy and sustainable transport technologies. In some circumstances these investments can act as a form of short-term economic stimulus, generating both jobs and incomes.[55] In the longer term technological and social innovation will need to drive very different patterns of production and consumption from those we see today, with much lower levels of energy and material use, and much higher levels of waste re-use and recycling.[56] We do not, if we are honest, know what impact this will have on long-term growth rates in developed countries.[57] But there is little reason to doubt that a highly productive, environmentally sustainable economy of this kind can generate a high standard of living, and one more fairly shared.[58] Indeed, it is now evident that the alternative – an environmentally unsustainable economy – will cause very serious damage to wellbeing and resilience in the medium and long term, particularly to those on the lowest and most vulnerable incomes.[59]

So going 'beyond growth' means neither abandoning growth as an objective nor relying upon it: it means changing the composition and structure of economic activity to achieve the multiple goals of a more rounded vision of economic and social progress. Policy making always involves difficult choices, particularly in the distribution of resources between groups and generations. But we are not compelled to make the same choices as those we have made in the past.

In recent years the terms 'inclusive growth' and 'green growth' have been used to describe national economic pathways aimed at meeting wider objectives of the kinds we suggest here. The OECD has taken an important lead in developing these ideas.[60] The comprehensive concept of 'sustainable development', embodied in the Sustainable Development Goals adopted by the United Nations, reflects the same impulse.[61] We are strongly supportive of these commitments. But it is also true that these terms can be used with a range of meanings, and have sometimes been accompanied by rather minimal policy changes in practice. As we discuss later in this report, the dynamics generating today's economic crises are deeply embedded in the structure of our economies. So giving serious priority to improving wellbeing, reducing inequalities, and achieving sustainability and resilience will demand more than a minor adjustment to current economic policies. Retrospective fiscal transfers, for example, are not sufficient to render economic growth 'inclusive'; deeper forms of structural change are required.[62] Environmental regulation is not of itself any guarantee of sustainability. The goals we set out here need to be *built in* to the design of policy.

There are three crucial dimensions to this process in practice. The first is the adoption of a wider set of primary economic indicators to guide policy making. It is now well known that GDP is not a good measure of overall economic performance. It does not take any account of the distribution of income and wealth; it captures only flows of income not the stocks of capital that generate them; it undervalues unpriced and intangible services; it ignores unpaid work; it fails to measure environmental degradation; it is not a good proxy for wellbeing.[63] Over the last decade the OECD's Better Life and Inclusive Growth Initiatives have therefore pioneered the development of economic indicators which better capture the multiple dimensions of economic and social progress, and a number of countries have begun to adopt them.[64] This involves use of a 'dashboard' of key indicators, including measurements of economic security, subjective wellbeing, environmental quality and public goods.[65] A particularly important new field is the development of 'distributional national accounts', which show not just the aggregate growth in GDP, but how it is distributed across income and population groups.[66]

But adoption of a set of indicators is not sufficient on its own. These have to become the accepted measures of the success of economic policy making. All too often governments have published sets of alternative indicators but then largely ignored them, both in making economic policy and in talking about it. For new indicators to be effective they must be communicated: politicians and policy makers (particularly in finance and economic ministries) must make clear in their public pronouncements that this is how they want economic performance to be judged, and media debate needs to reflect this. Going 'beyond growth' needs to be an explicit political aim, in turn reflected in a new public narrative and discourse on the nature of economic and social progress.[67]

Last, and most critically, the new economic indicators need to be attached to policies designed to improve them. It is no use adopting a new measure of performance, but then not having the mechanisms to influence it. This requires both an understanding of the causal factors which determine the level of the indicator; and the design of policies which can impact on it. It is for this reason that we argue in this report that policy makers need a deeper framework of understanding of how modern economies work, and the kinds of policies which can make them work more successfully. Multi-dimensional indicators require a more sophisticated menu of policies.

Most economic policy is made by national governments, but this process has a crucial international element too. In a globalised economy of complex supply chains and trading relationships, production and consumption patterns in one country powerfully impact on others, and many economic outcomes cannot be determined solely through national action. So there is a vital need to achieve new international agreements and co-ordination mechanisms in areas such as environmental degradation, labour standards and tax policy which can ensure that economic goals in one country are not met at the expense of others, and national policy is enhanced by international co-operation.[68]

New frameworks of economic analysis

Over a period of about thirty years up to the financial crisis of 2008, the dominant model of economic growth in developed countries rested, to a considerable extent, on a very particular form of neoclassical economic theory. This made relatively simple assumptions about how economic actors behave, and the implications of this for the functioning of the economy as a whole. In turn these led to a variety of standard prescriptions for economic policy which, while by no means universal, were widely adopted in both developed and developing countries.

It is important to note that this simple version of neoclassical theory was never universally accepted within academic economics. Indeed in most fields it was largely superseded by more complex approaches some time ago. But it is also true that it remains the standard framework for the teaching of economics at school and early undergraduate level,[69] and continues to be dominant in public discourse and commentary about economic policy.[70] And as an analytical framework it had a disproportionate influence on economic policy making in many countries for a long period.

At the heart of this theory was an assumption of 'rational' economic behaviour. Individuals maximised their utility, based on preferences formed outside of the economic process. Businesses sought to maximise their profits. The 'optimal' level of output and consumption (and wages and profits) would then be achieved in markets that were as competitive as possible. Where they were not, it should be the objective of policy to make them so. In fields as varied as labour market policy, financial markets and international trade (and in some countries in the provision of public services too), the dominant policy view was that markets should be liberalised if possible, thereby improving their efficiency and achieving the highest overall gain in output and welfare.

Orthodox neoclassical theory acknowledged the existence of 'market failure', where competitive markets do not produce optimal outcomes due to the existence of externalities (such as environmental degradation) or public goods (such as science or defence). Market failure justified a range of government interventions, from environmental taxes to the public provision of services such as education, policing and research and development. But the neoclassical framework also noted that governments can fail: states may be captured by the interests of their officials or politicians, or simply lack the knowledge or capacity to improve market behaviour. As a result, economic prescription based on simple neoclassical analysis tended to be sceptical about the role of government in trying to steer the economy towards ends other than those determined by existing markets and well-defined externalities.

At the level of the whole economy, most macroeconomic models before 2008 were constructed using the tools of neoclassical economics.[71] Such models typically assumed that households and businesses behave in homogeneous ways, so could be modelled as 'representative agents'. Though individual markets might involve frictions of various kinds, the long-run tendency of the economy was towards an equilibrium state, generally assumed to be at full employment. Instabilities were regarded as exogenous, coming from outside the system, rather than from within it. In macroeconomic policy, the neoclassical framework encouraged a view that high levels of government debt 'crowd out' private investment, so fiscal deficits should be limited, and monetary policy (adjustments to interest rates) should play the primary role in controlling inflation and managing overall demand.[72]

The relationship of theory to policy making was never straightforward. Academic economics has always been complex and varied, and policy never followed simply from theoretical analysis. Mainstream academic microeconomics began to move away from the simple neoclassical framework from the 1980s onwards, and plenty of economists have long rejected the standard policy prescriptions to which it gave rise. Nevertheless, the existence of a dominant paradigm in economic policy making and public discourse before 2008 is widely acknowledged, and its grounding in simple neoclassical theory evident.[73]

In the period since the financial crisis, however, the orthodox analysis underpinning economic policy has changed. In critical fields, from the crisis itself to the growth and impact of inequality, from the rise of environmental degradation to the slowdown in productivity growth, economists have had to acknowledge that the orthodox analytical framework has done a poor job of anticipating or explaining key developments, and have begun searching for more helpful approaches.[74]

It has been widely accepted, for example, that the crisis undermined the 'efficient markets hypothesis' which had previously informed financial deregulation.[75] It has become clear to both policy makers and economists, not least in international economic institutions and central banks, that the behaviour of the financial sector needs much more sophisticated analysis.[76] Indeed in a whole variety of areas, from the understanding of fragmented labour markets to the analysis of productivity differences between different kinds of firms, policy makers have had to acknowledge that actually-existing markets are *not* efficient, but beset by 'imperfections' and 'frictions' which require different kinds of policy solutions. In doing so they have effectively begun to catch up with many of the most important developments in mainstream academic economics of recent decades, such as the implications of information asymmetries between market actors in different kinds of economic transaction.[77] At the same time macroeconomic models have been modified to include different kinds of financial institutions and behaviour, and rigidities and shocks of various kinds.[78]

In turn, many economic policy institutions – including the OECD – have acknowledged the limitations and failures of the more simplistic free market prescriptions of the pre-crisis period. It has been generally accepted, for example, that financial regulation needs to go beyond individual firms to the systemic risks which the financial sector as a whole can generate. As a consequence, various forms of 'macroprudential regulation' are now being considered and implemented.[79] Similarly, it is now widely accepted that free trade and deeper integration into global markets can have persistent adverse consequences on particular groups of workers, sectors and geographical communities, and that counter-balancing policies are therefore needed.[80] In employment policy, minimum wages and active labour market policies to assist the unemployed into work (encompassing both education and training and welfare benefits) have been widely supported for some time, while other kinds of government intervention, such as to redress gender inequalities in work opportunities and pay, are also now widely advocated.[81]

These developments, and others like them, are welcome. But our view is that they have not yet gone far enough. For economics has been changing in more profound ways over recent decades. Across a whole range of issues, economists working in both mainstream and non-orthodox traditions – in many cases informed by other social sciences – have developed new theories and analytical frameworks which can better explain the way in which modern economies work, and why they often don't. Many of these frameworks, some of them reformulations of older theories, have good claims to provide a better fit with the evidence, and in turn greater explanatory power, than those which continue to dominate mainstream policy making and public discourse. As the empirical validity and theoretical value of these alternative approaches is increasingly recognised, the boundaries between 'mainstream' and 'heterodox' forms of economics are breaking down.[82] We list a few of the main developments here.[83]

Economic behaviour. Few economists now think that the idea of rational 'homo economicus' is a useful way of explaining how people behave in real economic life, despite its widespread continuing use. The field of behavioural economics, informed by experimental evidence in economic psychology, offers a more sophisticated way of understanding, and is increasingly being adopted in mainstream economic analysis.[84] People do not constantly calculate and optimise their welfare: they use various forms of 'bounded rationality'. To save the time and effort of calculation, many economic decisions are made using 'heuristics' and 'rules of thumb' of various kinds. At the same time, human reasoning is subject to many forms of bias. For example, people tend to operate within particular 'frames' of thought, rather than seeking a full range of information sources, and tend to draw general (and often mistaken) inferences from small samples of experience. 'Herd behaviour' (when people follow others' example, as happens, for example, in financial markets) can be common.

At the same time, economic psychologists and sociologists have emphasised the role of social influences on the formation of economic tastes and preferences.[85] People do not act solely in their own self-interest: they have strong attachments and moral views which lead to various forms of caring, co-operative and altruistic behaviour, as well as conformity to social norms. Such behaviours may not be subject to a calculative or individualistic logic at all: they suggest a 'social' human being as an important economic agent.[86] Economic action in this sense is powerfully 'embedded' in societal structures, institutions and relationships. Tastes and preferences are not somehow 'given', or exogenous to the economic system - they can be actively shaped by forces such as advertising, the impact of new technologies and new kinds of social networks and institutions. The narratives which are commonly told in society about how the economy works and how people behave in it themselves influence behaviour.[87]

Markets, institutions and power. The neoclassical idea of the competitive market was always intended to be a formalisation of what in the real world is obviously a wide range of different kinds of market arrangements. But over recent decades institutional and political economists of various kinds, working in both mainstream and heterodox traditions, have provided a more fundamental critique.[88] They have pointed out that markets are brought into being by institutions and the social rules they embody: by law, custom, social norms, the structure and ownership of businesses, by public policy. All of these – and therefore reforms to them – can change the ways in which different kinds of market operate, and the outcomes they generate. The idea of 'market competition' is simply too narrow a frame to understand this. Such economists have noted, for example, that the different systems of corporate governance and financing in different countries lead businesses to behave in different ways; that the relationship between corporations and governments is a vital element in understanding how markets work in practice; and that the development of digital information has fundamentally altered the nature of economic production. It is hard to understand the growth and business models of the new giant digital platform companies, for example, without these insights.[89] More widely, comparative political economists have sought to understand how markets are co-ordinated through different institutional arrangements in different countries, giving rise to distinctive 'varieties' of modern capitalism.[90]

Understanding markets as the outcome of the inter-relationships of institutions raises the inescapable issue of the role of power in the economy. The way in which today's labour markets work, for example, is made more explicable by analysing the relative power which employers, individual workers and groups of workers (organised for example in trade unions) have within them.[91] The growing concentration of many product markets in the hands of a small number of large corporations requires not just traditional analysis of monopoly and oligopoly, but of the impact of corporate lobbying on regulatory policy making. To understand the effect of rising inequality on economic outcomes requires an examination of the influence of the very wealthy on public policies such as taxation and public spending.[92] Overall, it forces attention to the interaction of the economy and economic policy with politics and systems of democracy.[93]

Evolution and complexity. The standard neoclassical idea of macroeconomics has an essentially timeless frame of reference: understood as a set of equilibrating markets, the economy is analysed with little reference to its own history or to the processes of change. This makes it difficult to comprehend why and how economies develop over time. Various kinds of evolutionary economists have sought to fill this gap.[94] They have shown how economies change in ways which mirror those of biological evolution, where differences in corporate behaviour and technological innovation generate advantages in markets and therefore get reproduced. They have analysed how change is 'path dependent', constrained by previous conditions and inertial forces. Many evolutionary economists and economic historians have focused on trying to understand innovation – the process of 'creative destruction' – as the key driving force of economic growth over time.[95] They have explained innovation as an institutional process influenced not just by the processes of technological 'invention' within firms, but the wider system of 'innovation networks' and financial markets, and the often powerful role of public funding at various points in the innovation process.[96]

The dynamics of innovation are hard to reconcile with the neoclassical view of the economy as an essentially equilibrating system: in reality it is always in turbulent flux. The school of complexity economics has sought to combine this insight with those of behavioural and institutional economics to understand the economy as a complex, adaptive system.[97] Drawing on the modern systems theory developed to analyse complex systems in biology and engineering, complexity economics seeks to understand the ways in which the multiple and non-linear relationships between heterogeneous actors in a modern economy generate aggregate outcomes which are not simply the sum or average of their constituent parts. Complex systems result in new, 'emergent' outcomes which cannot be predicted through a mechanistic approach based simply on their micro-foundations. Understanding this has particular value to elucidate complex systems such as finance and global value chains. Complexity economists have developed new kinds of 'agent-based' models which abandon the assumptions of rationality, representative agents, optimising behaviour and equilibrium of the standard neoclassical model. Utilising the new availability of big data and modern computing power, such models are able to represent the economy in more complex ways, offering the potential of better explanation and prediction.[98]

Finance and macroeconomics. The failure of most macroeconomists to predict the financial crash of 2008, and the continued weakness of many developed economies despite the very low interest rates of the last decade, have led to a fundamental reassessment of neoclassically-based theory. A crucial dimension of this has focused on the role of the financial sector. Prior to the crash financial regulation was largely based on the neoclassical 'efficient markets hypothesis', which assumed that, with near-perfect information, liberalised financial markets would generate an optimal allocation of resources.[99] The evident failure of this theory has renewed interest in 'post-Keynesian' analysis which explains how financial markets shift between stability and fragility, and their tendency to create asset bubbles and subsequent crises.[100] As the 'financialisation' of many economies has increased, economists are analysing the impacts which different kinds of financial actors and assets have on economic performance: the role of speculative and short-term financial trading, for example; the critical role played by investment in real estate; and the rise of the 'shadow banking' system.[101]

At the same time Keynesian and post-Keynesian economists have challenged the neoclassical orthodoxy around fiscal and monetary policy. Such economists emphasise the importance of effective aggregate demand in determining productivity and output growth, and the central role played by uncertainty in economic behaviour.[102] They have focused on the role of fiscal policy in stimulating growth (in part through its effect on business expectations), and the limitations (and inequitable impacts) of monetary policy. Such insights are indeed now being partially accepted in 'mainstream' economic analysis: it is now widely argued, for example, that a more active fiscal policy is both necessary and desirable in present conditions when interest rates are very low and monetary policy has largely run out of options.[103] Contrary to neoclassical orthodoxy, it has been shown how high levels of public borrowing and debt can be sustained so long as the growth rate of the economy (which can itself be stimulated by public investment) exceeds the rate of interest paid.[104] Public investment can 'crowd in', rather than 'crowd out', private finance.[105] Post-Keynesian economists have shown how money is created 'endogenously' by commercial bank lending, rather than by central banks.[106] Some (working within 'modern monetary theory') have indeed questioned the entire basis of monetary policy, proposing the use of monetary financing ('printing money') to finance public spending.[107]

A key field has been the development of new kinds of macroeconomic models. The unrealistic assumptions and poor predictive performance of standard 'dynamic stochastic general equilibrium' (DSGE) models used by many central banks and finance ministries has led to a questioning of their neoclassical 'micro-foundations', such as rational expectations and representative agents.[108] The new models incorporate financial assets of various kinds, can better account for the impact of stocks as well as flows, and allow for more realistic behavioural and institutional assumptions, including the critical role of information asymmetries and uncertainty, and the possibility of endogenous shocks and structural breaks in economic evolution, such as financial crises.[109]

The natural environment. Neoclassical economics understands environmental degradation as a form of market failure, where environmental goods are unpriced. It therefore seeks to find a monetary value for environmental resources or the damage caused to them, and to use environmental taxes or other incentive mechanisms (such as tradable permit systems) to 'internalise' the external cost and so correct the market failure.[110] But this approach cannot fully explain or address the prevalence of environmental degradation. Ecological economists have offered a more fundamental explanation.[111] They have shown how the economy is in reality a subset of the earth's biophysical systems: it depends on the natural environment to provide it with resources, assimilate its wastes, and to provide various life support services such as nutrient recycling and climatic regulation. These processes are governed by the laws of thermodynamics, which ensure that all resources are turned back into wastes, in a more 'entropic', or disordered (and therefore often polluting), state. Natural systems do not behave in linear ways but exhibit a range of thresholds and 'tipping points' which, when exceeded, risk catastrophic change, sometimes to local environments, sometimes (as with climate change) to the global one.

For these reasons, ecological economics seeks to bring the economy back within the earth's 'sustainability limits' or 'planetary boundaries', where environmental systems can naturally regenerate.[112] This will involve, not the marginal changes assumed by the notion of market failure, but transformation in the environmental structures of modern economies: the use of carbon-based energy, car-based cities, intensive agriculture, and the over-exploitation of soil, forests and fisheries. A wide range of policy instruments will be required to stimulate this, including, but going well beyond, environmental taxes.[113] This will have powerful implications for macroeconomic policy: the notion of economic growth itself will need re-evaluating.[114]

Inequality. As inequality has grown in recent years, a growing number of economists have sought to map its extent, and understand both its causes and its effects.[115] In doing so they have challenged some of the fundamental tenets of the standard neoclassical approach. For example, it has become clear that the increasing liberalisation of international trade does not have the widespread economic benefits formerly assumed, particularly for already open economies. Although greater trade may raise GDP, it frequently results in a highly uneven distribution of the benefits, with significant net economic costs being borne by particular industrial sectors and the geographic communities dependent on them.[116] Actual experience in a variety of countries suggests that a non-liberalised, more government-directed approach to trade and industrial policy may have a much stronger impact on growth and its distribution.[117]

As already noted, one of the key trends of the last forty years in many developed countries has been the declining proportion of national income which has gone to wages and salaries (the 'labour share') and the rising share going to the owners of land and capital.[118] This has been explained in terms of the rising returns to capital (both of land and business profits) relative to the growth rate of the economy as a whole, and of the increasing ability of higher income groups to capture the unearned 'rents' or surpluses from economic activity.[119] The relative power of employers and workers in the labour markets for different kinds of work has then magnified the difference in earnings between workers in different occupations.[120] Rising inequality has been shown to have powerfully negative impacts on the wider economy, including on productivity and economic growth and on many indicators of individual and social wellbeing.[121]

Gender. One of the persistent dimensions of inequality has been by gender. Women in all countries are systematically under-represented in high-status and high-earnings occupations, and over-represented in low-status, low-income ones.[122] A strong tradition of research in labour market economics has sought to understand the interaction of gender, family and labour supply.[123] Feminist economists have gone further, seeking to locate such gender stratification in the deeper structures in society which entrench the relative roles and power of men and women.[124] Comparable analyses have examined how ethnic minorities also experience systematic discrimination and under-representation in higher-status and higher-income occupations, the basis of this in the colonial and slavery histories of western economies, and the ways in which inequalities of gender, race and class intersect.[125] Analysis of economic and public policy outcomes without understanding their gender and racial dimensions is simply incomplete.

A critical feature of feminist economics has been an expansion of the boundaries of the economy and of economic analysis. It has emphasised the critical role which the unpaid work of raising children, very largely done by women, plays in maintaining the processes and structures of society ('social reproduction'), and the way this is systematically ignored in mainstream economic accounting and analysis. This is also true of other forms of unpaid work, such as caring for elderly and disabled people and voluntary and community work of various kinds. Only by understanding the economic value produced by these activities, it is argued, can the functioning of the economy, and its embeddedness in social structures and relations, be properly understood.[126]

Ethics and the role of the state. Inequality in its various dimensions forces a questioning of the ethical basis of economic analysis. Proponents of the standard neoclassical framework widely assume it to be ethically neutral, since it seeks to maximise welfare given the existing tastes and preferences of consumers; it does not judge these.[127] But in practice those tastes and preferences are highly dependent on the distribution of income. Since people's tastes and preferences change as they move along the income scale, a different distribution would generate a different pattern of economic activity. This is even before we consider the moral claims of future generations.[128] So regarding the maximization of welfare under current conditions as ethically 'neutral' is in practice to accept the current distribution of income (including between generations). It is for this reason that economic philosophers and political economists have argued for a more honest understanding of the inescapably ethical character of economic analysis. In turn this would lead to a more sophisticated public debate about the justice (or otherwise) of different economic arrangements and policies.[129]

It also suggests a re-examination of the role of the state in economic policy. The neoclassical framework presupposes that well-functioning markets optimise overall welfare, and government policy is therefore justified to correct market failures. But if public policy is to aim at different ethical outcomes, the state will have to play a larger role in guiding, or steering, the overall patterns of economic activity to achieve them. Through public service and welfare provision it can also support a fairer and more productive form of economic development. 'Correcting market failures' will not be sufficient; markets can also be 'shaped' in pursuit of publicly-determined goals.[130]

These developments in economics and political economy over recent years (and this does not claim to be a complete account) have generated important new understandings of how modern economies work, and they have been widely backed by new empirical evidence.[131] Many recent Nobel Memorial Prizes in Economics have been awarded to the leading exponents in these fields.[132] At the same time, the advent of new data sources has enabled economics to become a much more empirical social science.[133] It is notable that some of the key insights have arisen both within mainstream economic traditions – by relaxing simplistic assumptions and introducing 'frictions' or new explanatory variables of various kinds – and in more explicitly 'heterodox' ones.[134] In the former case the core frameworks of mainstream economics have been retained but modified; in the latter a more radical revision is sought.[135] But between them the result is that economic analysis and policy making are now able to draw upon a much richer and more empirically-based menu of academic economics and political economy than has generally been used or featured in public discourse over the last thirty years or so. Economics teaching has begun (in some places) to be reformed, with new curricula emphasising non-orthodox approaches to analysing economic problems and policies.[136]

There is no single synthetic theory which has emerged from these different approaches to economic thought. But this is not because they offer fundamentally competing analyses. Indeed in many cases there are strong synergies between them, and powerful ways in which they can be combined. Post-Keynesian macroeconomic models, for example, incorporate a variety of institutional economic insights. Policy aimed at transforming the economic structures which generate environmental unsustainability is gaining from the approach of evolutionary and innovation economists to industrial strategy. Insights from behavioural economics have been important for understanding how financial markets work in practice. Gender analysis has deepened other analyses of inequality. All economic policy making will be enhanced by a clearer understanding of the distribution of power in the way economic decisions are made.

Many economists working in the complexity field have been explicit in making these links and incorporating insights from a wide range of economic analyses. Since their aim has been to understand in a more sophisticated way how economic agents behave and the outcomes which emerge from their interactions, they have used a range of economic approaches which can help illuminate these.[137] The broad field of political economy likewise encompasses a range of interdisciplinary approaches, drawing on critical insights from history, sociology, anthropology and other fields.[138]

Over the last decade much economic policy making and advice has moved away from the simple 'orthodox' approach which was dominant in the period before the financial crisis. But the persistence of serious economic problems, and the rise of new challenges, suggests that this movement has not yet gone far enough. Similarly, the new frameworks of economic thought we have presented here are already present in mainstream economics, in some cases blurring the lines between the mainstream and the heterodox. But again, this has not yet gone far enough. Our view is that these two shifts need to be harnessed to one another. The new modes of economic analysis can provide a much broader approach to economic policy making than the simple neoclassical framework. They can help explain why conventional policies have not been working well in addressing the multiple challenges faced by OECD countries. And in turn they can help point the way to alternatives that might more successfully do so. There is considerable scope to utilise the new economics in pursuit of more successful policy

New approaches to economic policy

As the multiple problems and challenges facing developed economies have emerged over the last decade, many new approaches to economic policy have been developed in response. These have sought to contribute to the new goals of economic policy making proposed in this report, with many drawing on the new frameworks of economic analysis described above. Some have been developed and are already being implemented by governments; some are under discussion within the OECD; others have been put forward by academic research institutes, think tanks and other organisations in civil society.[139] We highlight a few examples here which illustrate some of the core themes of this report. These are in no sense intended to be comprehensive. In each case there is much further work to be done to refine and tailor them to the particular circumstances of individual countries.

These approaches reflect two key insights. The first is that the deep challenges facing OECD economies today will not be addressed simply by incremental changes to existing policies. Environmental unsustainability, low levels of investment and slow productivity growth, rising inequality, the power of monopoly corporations, growing financialisation, accelerating automation: each of these arises from structural features of modern economies. So they will require a more profound shift in the kinds of policy which governments use to address them.

For much of the last forty years, the dominant approach to economic policy making in most OECD countries has been to focus on the 'supply side' of the economy – attempting to ensure that economic conditions such as infrastructure provision, competition and regulatory policy, and the education and incentives of the labour force, are supportive of private sector investment and growth. Macroeconomic policy has been aimed at the control of inflation. At the same time, some of the adverse impacts of growth have been ameliorated 'after the fact' by redistributing income through the tax and benefit system, and though various forms of social and environmental policy. Meanwhile the central engine of the economy – the patterns of investment and forms of production that generate its shape, direction and scale – have been largely left to be determined by private sector businesses and finance.

Though both supply side and ameliorative policies are still extremely important, we believe they are no longer sufficient to address today's economic challenges. We need to pay attention to the way the engine itself works. For it is in the patterns of investment and forms of production themselves that the major problems and challenges arise. If we are to achieve the new economic goals we have set out - environmental sustainability, improved wellbeing, a reduction in inequality, and greater resilience - these need to be built into the structures of the economy from the outset, not simply hoped for as a by-product, or added after the event.

Second, it is vital that policy is made in an integrated way. This starts from the adoption of economic performance and wellbeing indicators which capture the full breadth of economic and social objectives. But as we noted earlier, this in itself is not sufficient. These indicators must then be attached to policies which can change how they perform – not just individually, but together. Multiple objectives can only be achieved if economic and social policy making moves out of its traditional silos and seeks out the synergies as well as the trade-offs between different policy areas.[140] We cannot, for example, achieve environmental sustainability in ways which simply exacerbate inequalities. Reform of the financial system to reduce systemic risk must also distribute wealth more broadly. Macroeconomic policy must be bounded by environmental sustainability limits. Overall public spending must be audited for its impact on each of the multiple dimensions of wellbeing. Policy must take account of international as well as domestic impacts. Institutional innovation in government will therefore be widely required. None of this is easy; but we will fail the challenges we confront unless it is done.

Sustainability and decarbonisation policy poses perhaps the most acute and urgent challenge in these respects. In the past, environmental policy has been aimed at improving the impacts of specific products and production activities – through regulatory measures such as energy efficiency and pollution standards and protection of natural areas. But it is evident that these have not been enough to drive aggregate environmental degradation – especially but not only greenhouse gas emissions – down to sustainable levels. So policy makers must now consider how long-term decarbonisation and sustainability targets can be given greater legal and economic force, and used to drive investment and production into more sustainable and resilient forms.[141] This will involve detailed examination not just of the technological options which can achieve radically lower environmental impact (in sectors such as energy, transport, buildings, agriculture and industry) but the patterns of consumption and modes of living which will be associated with them.[142] Some activities – the subsidy of fossil fuels, for example – will evidently need to cease,[143] while 'just transition' strategies will be required to ensure an equitable restructuring of carbon-intensive sectors and enable workers to retrain for new jobs.[144] To make choices of these kinds, it seems clear that governments will need to engage in much deeper forms of sectoral planning, social partnership and public consultation than most have practised in the recent past.

Innovation and industrial policy will then have to play a crucial role. Over the last few years a number of governments and public institutions have taken up the idea of 'mission-oriented' innovation and industrial policy.[145] This starts from the insight that economic development has a *direction* as well as a rate. So public policy can help drive innovation into meeting the major environmental and social challenges our societies face – such as decarbonisation, environmental sustainability, health and social care, and digital inclusion. Using a combination of policy targets, public procurement, innovation spending and 'patient' public investment, a more active industrial policy can help steer the economy, not just to support stronger industrial performance (with benefits to job creation, trade and regional growth) but social and environmental goals as well. In most countries a strongly devolved regional policy (including, for example, 'community wealth-building' initiatives at local level[146]) will be necessary to ensure more equitable geographical outcomes.

There is a strong case for a more active industrial policy to be supported by a more active ***macroeconomic policy***. With real interest rates still very low and quantitative easing still in place, many economists and economic institutions now accept that fiscal policy will be needed to ensure sufficient aggregate demand to create new jobs, particularly in the face of a global downturn.[147] Although public debt levels remain high in many countries, it is now widely recognised that public borrowing for investment which supports economic growth (in, for example, infrastructure, innovation and public services) can be sustainable, paying for itself over time.[148] It is notable that many public investments which support growth and job creation will also contribute to improved individual wellbeing, and social cohesion and solidarity.

Improving the resilience of the economy through stronger ***financial regulation*** remains an important priority. Though the period since the financial crash has seen stricter regulation of individual financial institutions, many analysts warn that the financial system as a whole remains fragile.[149] While policy makers have been developing new forms of macro-prudential regulation aimed at preventing excessive credit growth, it is not clear that these are yet strong enough to prevent another crisis, with the growth of the largely unregulated shadow banking system a particular concern.[150] In some countries there have been calls to limit the overall size of the financial sector, to control its adverse impacts on pay and asset inequality, currency appreciation and the attraction of talent.[151] So there are strong grounds for exploring stricter regulation of the types of assets which financial institutions can hold, penalising (through regulation or taxation) various forms of high carbon, speculative and 'non-productive' financial activity, and incentivising long-term investment in productive sectors of the economy.[152] In some countries this might include reforms to the 'shareholder value' model of ***corporate governance*** and executive pay, which it is widely argued has encouraged an excessive focus on short-term returns and a decline in long-term investment.[153]

More widely, there is increasing interest in the role which reform of ***competition policy*** might play in regulating the growth of companies with powerful monopoly positions, particularly in key digital markets. While different countries have different competition regimes, the orthodox approach of judging competition and market power largely through their impact on consumer prices has come under increasing challenge.[154] With expanding influence on many aspects of life, from the media and privacy to the development of artificial intelligence, the structure and regulation of digital platform companies is a particular focus of policy concern. This will clearly have to be done on an international as well as national basis.[155] At the same time there is increasing scrutiny of the ways in which multinational corporations govern their global supply chains, particularly in relation to issues such as labour and environmental standards.[156] Raising such standards through new forms of ***international trade agreements*** offers a potentially powerful approach.[157] Co-ordinating ***corporate taxation*** regimes on an international basis to ensure that multinational corporations pay fair levels of taxation in the countries in which they operate (for example by allocating global profits proportionately to national sales) will also be important.[158]

Building dynamics to reduce inequality into the structures and institutions of the economy poses a real challenge to policy makers. While redistributive measures through the fiscal and welfare systems remain vital, not least to combat persistent poverty, it also requires 'predistributive' measures that address inequality's complex drivers.[159] One of these lies in the **ownership of wealth**, which in many countries has become more concentrated over the last decade.[160] A variety of approaches to spreading wealth more widely are now under discussion in many places, including mechanisms to broaden the ownership of companies, reforms to land ownership and housing markets and the design of 'citizen's wealth funds'.[161] It is also widely argued that wealth, and income from wealth, need to be better taxed.[162] Reducing inequality will require particular attention paid to **labour market policies**. The falling share of national income going into wages and salaries (relative to capital) over recent decades has reflected a decline in the effective bargaining power of workers, particularly in lower-skilled jobs. Reversing this would require a range of kinds of measures: raising minimum wages; improving the access of trade unions to workers, particularly in smaller firms and under-unionised sectors; improving the regulation of working conditions and contracts, particularly in the so-called 'gig economy' of precarious work; employee profit-sharing schemes; improving the provision of childcare; and increasing the role of collective bargaining, particularly at a sectoral level.[163]

Collective bargaining will be particularly important to steer and manage the processes of **automation**, ensuring that the benefits of higher productivity do not accrue simply to the owners of capital, but also to employees.[164] As the processes of both automation and decarbonisation have the effect of redistributing employment opportunities, there is increasing interest in the role of government 'job guarantees' to smooth the transition.[165] 'Flexicurity' welfare policies which combine flexibility for employers with income security for workers may also be important.[166] There is growing interest in some circles in the idea of a 'universal basic income' for the same reason.[167] Others propose a system of 'universal basic services', including education, healthcare, housing and transport.[168] Systematic measures will be needed to end discrimination against women, ethnic minorities and other minority groups in many countries, and to increase investment in childcare and early years provision. Investment in lifelong education and skills training will become increasingly vital.[169] Perhaps more radically, there is increasing interest in the potential of reducing working hours to capture the gains of higher productivity in improved wellbeing, rather than simply higher consumption.[170]

The aim of each of these kinds of policy approaches – and this is not, of course, an exhaustive list – is to help shift the structure of economies so that their internal dynamics work towards the goals of environmental sustainability, improved wellbeing, declining inequality and greater resilience. Rather than bolting on policies which have to act *against* the dominant dynamics of the economic system, the aim should be to change the way the engine of the economy works, so that these goals are its primary outcomes.

This must extend beyond the domestic to the international sphere. In a complex, interconnected global economy, it is not possible for individual countries to achieve economic and social progress in isolation. Global, multilateral rules are needed to prevent financial crises, tackle tax evasion and money laundering, address the global character of climate change and environmental degradation, regulate labour standards in international supply chains, and shift the distribution of global resources towards the poorest countries and people. A new global governance regime is urgently required.[171]

We are under no illusions as to how easy or quick policy changes of these kinds will be. They will require significant institutional reform. Many vested interests will stand in the way – the resistance of those with incumbent economic power is of course a major reason why more equitable and sustainable policies have not been followed over the last decade and longer. So we recognise that this is as much a political as an economic policy making challenge. In some countries it may require innovations in democratic practice and the ways in which policy is made, for example to open it up to wider consultation and participation.[172]

It may also require a new role for the state. In recent years a number of practitioners and commentators have sought to explore how modern governments can offer more than safety nets for their citizens, providing them with assets and skills that do not simply remove barriers to opportunities, but furnish people with the capacity to seize them.[173] At the same time states must become more entrepreneurial, seeking to shape markets and steer the process of economic change, not simply correct market failures. An empowering and entrepreneurial state of this kind would allow the development of a new kind of social contract – a new relationship between the state, business, civil society and citizens.[174] It will be hard to manage the processes of decarbonisation and automation, for example, without such an explicit understanding of how the risks and benefits will be shared. These processes will take a different form in every country – despite the processes of globalisation, every country retains its own history, cultures and institutions and there is no one model which fits all. But everywhere it will without doubt need political imagination and courage.

Conclusion

If the world is to address the profound challenges and problems which confront us today, 'business as usual' is not an option. In a world of extraordinary complexity and radical uncertainty, only the foolish would argue that the solutions are simple. But this does not mean that it is beyond the capacity of our societies to find them.

A decade ago the financial crisis rocked not just the world's economic system, but the confidence that policy makers knew how to manage it. In the decade since, important changes have been made. Economic analysis has become more sophisticated, and new approaches have been adopted in policy making and advice – many of them led by the OECD.

But the depth of the issues we now face makes clear that these processes have not yet gone far enough. Though modified and improved, policy makers are essentially still operating with the pre-crisis economic framework and its accompanying forms of policy. We believe that more radical rethinking is required.

In this report we have tried to set out how this can be done. It encompasses a new set of goals and measures of economic and social progress; new frameworks of economic analysis; and new kinds of policies.

These are not new in the sense of 'original': on the contrary, a critical part of our argument is that what we are doing is bringing together well-established ideas which have many authors and important intellectual histories. But we do claim that it offers an alternative to the approach to economic policy making which has been dominant in OECD countries over the last forty or so years. If the new goals we propose are to be achieved, a new model of economic and social development is needed.

The critical idea – the common thread – that runs through our argument is that economics and economic policy need properly to understand the sociality of human life. People are not the individual utility maximisers of orthodox economic myth: they have multi-dimensional preferences and ethics formed in social and cultural settings. So there is a reflexive interaction between individual economic decisions and societal forces, working itself out in social institutions and through political processes. This means that our conception of economic progress needs to extend beyond individual, material prosperity to include indicators of social wellbeing, cohesion and empowerment, and the environmental boundaries of human activity. Our frameworks of economic analysis need to acknowledge the social, historical, political and environmental context of economic behaviour, and the feedback loops between individual decisions and societal dynamics which characterise economic systems. Our approach to policy must go beyond the traditional instruments of economic policy to encompass reform of institutions, social policy and political narratives.

We make no claim that what we have presented is a fully-fledged and coherent model of economic and social development which can simply be taken off the shelf and implemented. Much more work needs to be done. Yet it is evident too that many of these ideas have already begun to enter mainstream economic and political debate, even if their full implications have not yet been acknowledged. The OECD, particularly through its New Approaches to Economic Challenges initiative, has played an important role in these processes. The task now, in our view, is to move from debate to practice.

It is daunting for economic policy makers to contemplate a fundamental shift in the way they make policy. But this kind of change has happened twice before in the last century.[175] In the 1940s, in the aftermath of the Wall Street Crash and the Great Depression, the economic orthodoxy of *laissez faire*, which had dominated analysis and policy making in the preceding period, was replaced. Keynesian economic theory provided a better way of understanding how economies could be revived, and the economic policies of full employment and the welfare state won broad support across the political spectrum. But the 'post-war consensus' itself broke down amid the economic crises of the 1970s, and it too was replaced. The free market or 'neoliberal' model developed by economists such as Milton Friedman and Friedrich Hayek appeared to offer a better economic analysis, and a more dynamic policy prescription. Adopted originally (and most fully) by the US and UK under the governments of Ronald Reagan and Margaret Thatcher, the market-oriented model in various forms came to be applied widely across the OECD in the subsequent decades.

Social scientists describe these moments of economic change as 'paradigm shifts' – periods when old orthodoxies are unable either to explain or to provide policy solutions to conditions of crisis, and new approaches take their place.[176] More than a decade after the financial crash, with the global economy and many individual OECD countries facing multiple crises, our argument is that the time is ripe for another such paradigm shift. The frameworks and prescriptions which have dominated policy making in recent decades are no longer able to generate the solutions to the problems and challenges we face today. We need a less incremental, more profound form of change.

This will not be easy. No single prescription will fit all circumstances. Every country is different, and each will wish to find its own way. But we are struck by the wealth of insight and understanding which now exists across the field of academic economics and economic policy making, from which solutions can be drawn. We believe the OECD has a critical role to play in stimulating understanding and debate about these new approaches. We applaud the OECD for its vital work in this field over recent years, and strongly recommend it continues to engage its member states and the wider global economic and political community to discuss and shape these new approaches further, and to support their implementation. The prize could not be greater.

Notes

1 Global Preparedness Monitoring Board (2019), *A World at Risk: Annual Report on Global Preparedness for Health Emergencies*. https://apps.who.int/gpmb/assets/annual_report/GPMB_annualreport_2019.pdf

2 *Financial Times* (2020), Will coronavirus pandemic finally kill off global supply chains? 28 May https://www.ft.com/content/4ee0817a-809f-11ea-b0fb-13524ae1056b

3 *Financial Times* (2020), 'Deprived areas hit hardest in UK by pandemic', 1 May https://www.ft.com/content/c26434a2-5337-45e9-a94b-2c33fd55306a. Sanchez-Paramo, C. (2020) 'Covid-19 will hit the poor hardest. Here's what we can do about it', World Bank blog, 23 April. https://blogs.worldbank.org/voices/covid-19-will-hit-poor-hardest-heres-what-we-can-do-about-it

4 World Economic Forum (2020), '11,000 deaths avoided during lockdown in Europe – thanks to cleaner air', 11 May https://www.weforum.org/agenda/2020/05/coronavirus-lockdown-cuts-air-pollution-deaths-avoided/

5 Ilzetzki, E. (2020). 'How worrying is Britain's debt? Surprisingly, we economists say: not very', *The Guardian*, 12 June https://www.theguardian.com/commentisfree/2020/jun/12/britain-public-debt-economists-coronavirus-deficit-austerity

6 IPCC (2018). *Special Report on Global Warming of 1.5°C*. Intergovernmental Panel on Climate Change https://www.ipcc.ch/sr15/

7 UNEP (2019), *Global Environment Outlook 6*. UN Environment Programme.https://www.unenvironment.org/resources/global-environment-outlook-6. Intergovernmental Science-Policy Platform on Biodiversity and Ecosystem Services (2019), *Global Assessment Report on Biodiversity and Ecosystem Services*. https://www.ipbes.net/global-assessment-report-biodiversity-ecosystem-services

8 http://www.oecd.org/employment/future-of-work/

9 OECD (2019), *An Introduction to Online Platforms and Their Role in the Digital Transformation*, OECD Publishing. https://doi.org/10.1787/53e5f593-en. OECD (2017), *OECD Digital Economy Outlook 2017*, OECD Publishing. http://dx.doi.org/10.1787/9789264276284-en. Zuboff, S. (2019) *The Age of Surveillance Capitalism*. PublicAffairs / Profile Books.

10 Helbing, D. (ed) (2019). *Towards Digital Enlightenment*. Springer. Margolis, M. and Moreno-Riaño, G. (2016). *The Prospect of Internet Democracy*. Routledge. O'Keeffe, G. S., and Clarke-Pearson, K. (2011). The impact of social media on children, adolescents, and families. *Pediatrics*, 127 (4), 800-804

11 World Bank and World Trade Organization (2019). *Global Value Chain Development Report 2019: Technological Innovation, Supply Chain Trade, and Workers in a Globalized World*, World Bank Group.http://documents.worldbank.org/curated/en/384161555079173489/Global-Value-Chain-Development-Report-2019-Technological-Innovation-Supply-Chain-Trade-and-Workers-in-a-Globalized-World

12 Cournède, B., Denk. O. and Hoeller, P. (2015), *Finance and Inclusive Growth*, OECD Economic Policy Papers, No. 14, OECD Publishing. https://doi.org/10.1787/5js06pbhf28s-en

13 Agénor, P. R. and Pereira da Silva, L. A. (2019). Global banking, financial spillovers, and macroprudential policy coordination. *BIS Working Papers* No 764. https://www.bis.org/publ/work764.htm. Buchak, G. et al. (2018). Fintech, regulatory arbitrage, and the rise of shadow banks. *Journal of Financial Economics*, 130 (3), 453-483.

14 OECD (2019). Adapting to demographic change. Paper prepared for the G20 Employment Working Group, 25-27 February 2019, Tokyo. http://www.oecd.org/g20/summits/osaka/OECD-Ageing-and-Demographic-change-G20-JPN.pdf. OECD (2018), *International Migration Outlook 2018*, OECD Publishing. https://doi.org/10.1787/migr_outlook-2018-en.

15 OECD (2019), *OECD Economic Outlook*, Volume 2019 Issue 1. OECD Publishing. https://doi.org/10.1787/b2e897b0-en

16 OECD (2019). OECD National Accounts Statistics (database). https://doi.org/10.1787/data-00619-en; https://doi.org/10.1787/f54eea03-en

17 OECD (2019). *OECD Economic Outlook, Volume 2019 Issue 1*. OECD Publishing. https://doi.org/10.1787/5713bd7d-en. OECD (2015), *The Future of Productivity*, OECD Publishing. https://www.oecd.org/eco/OECD-2015-The-future-of-productivity-book.pdf

18 Alvaredo, F. et al. (eds.) (2018). *World Inequality Report 2018*. Belknap Press. https://wir2018.wid.world/files/download/wir2018-full-report-english.pdf

19 OECD (2019), 'Unemployment rate' (indicator), https://doi.org/10.1787/997c8750-en (accessed on 08 July 2019). OECD (2019), 'Youth unemployment rate' (indicator), https://doi.org/10.1787/c3634df7-en (accessed on 08 July 2019).

20 OECD (2019), *OECD Employment Outlook 2019: The Future of Work*, OECD Publishing. https://doi.org/10.1787/9ee00155-en.

21 OECD (2018), *OECD Employment Outlook 2018*, OECD Publishing. https://doi.org/10.1787/empl_outlook-2018-en. OECD (2019), *Under Pressure: The Squeezed Middle Class*, OECD Publishing. https://doi.org/10.1787/689afed1-en

22 Ibid.

23 OECD (2017), *Trust and Public Policy: How Better Governance Can Help Rebuild Public Trust*, OECD Public Governance Reviews, OECD Publishing. https://doi.org/10.1787/9789264268920-en

24 Ibid.

25 World Bank. GovData 306 Social cohesion (trust in others).https://govdata360.worldbank.org/subtopics/hfd8e0e0f

26 Snower, D. J. (2018). Beyond capital and wealth. *Economics*, 12 (2018-21), 1-10.

27 Rodrik, D. (2018). Populism and the economics of globalization. *Journal of International Business Policy*, 1-22. https://doi.org/10.1057/s42214-018-0001-4. Hopkin, J., and Blyth, M. (2019). The global economics of European populism: growth regimes and party system change in Europe. *Government and Opposition*, 54 (2), 193-225. https://doi.org/10.1017/gov.2018.43

28 Teulings, C and Baldwin, R. (eds) (2014). Secular Stagnation: Facts, Causes and Cures. Vox/CEPR. https://voxeu.org/content/secular-stagnation-facts-causes-and-cures

29 *The Economist* (2018). The next recession. 11 October. https://www.economist.com/leaders/2018/10/11/the-next-recession

30 OECD (2019). *Going Digital: Shaping Policies, Improving Lives*. OECD Publishing. https://www.oecd.org/going-digital/going-digital-shaping-policies-improving-lives-9789264312012-en.htm. Unger, R. M (2019), *The Knowledge Economy*. Verso. Haskel, J. and Westlake, S. (2017). *Capitalism Without Capital: The Rise of the Intangible Economy*. Princeton University Press.

31 IMF (2018). *Global Financial Stability Report 2018*. International Monetary Fund. https://www.imf.org/en/Publications/GFSR/Issues/2018/09/25/Global-Financial-Stability-Report-October-2018

32 Williamson, J. (2004). A short history of the Washington Consensus. Peterson Institute for International Economics. https://www.piie.com/publications/papers/williamson0204.pdf

33 Ostry, J. D., Loungani, P. and Ferceri, D. (2016). Neoliberalism: Oversold? *IMF Finance and Development* 53 (2), 38-41. https://www.imf.org/external/pubs/ft/fandd/2016/06/pdf/ostry.pdf

34 https://www.oecd.org/naec/

35 OECD (2018). *Elements for a New Growth Narrative. Draft Report*. http://www.oecd.org/naec/SG_NAEC(2018)1_Elements%20for%20a%20new%20growth%20narrative.pdf. OECD (2017). *New Approaches to Economic Challenges Towards a New Narrative*. Consultation draft. http://www.oecd.org/naec/OSG%20NAEC%20Forum%20report.pdf. OECD (2015). Final NAEC Synthesis New Approaches to Economic Challenges. http://www.oecd.org/mcm/documents/Final-NAEC-Synthesis-Report-CMIN2015-2.pdf. OECD (2014). *New Approaches to Economic Challenges (NAEC) Synthesis*. http://www.oecd.org/mcm/C-MIN(2014)2-ENG.pdf. OECD (2013). *New Approaches to Economic Challenges (NAEC) Summary and Update*. http://www.oecd.org/mcm/C-MIN%282013%2923-ENG.pdf.

36 UNCTAD (2012). *Trade and Development Report 2012*. Chapter 3: Evolution of income inequality: different time perspectives and dimensions. UN Conference on Trade and Development. https://unctad.org/en/PublicationChapters/tdr2012ch3_en.pdf

37 Dinda, S. (2004). Environmental Kuznets curve hypothesis: a survey. *Ecological Economics*, 49 (4), 431-455.

38 Dao, M. C. et al. (2017). Drivers of declining labor share of income. IMFBlog. https://blogs.imf.org/2017/04/12/drivers-of-declining-labor-share-of-income/

39 World Inequality Database. https://wid.world/world/#sptinc_p90p100_z/US;FR;DE;CN;ZA;GB;WO/last/eu/k/p/yearly/s/false/25.253500000000003/80/curve/false/country. Alvaredo, F. et al. (eds.). (2018). *World Inequality Report 2018*. Belknap Press. https://wir2018.wid.world/files/download/wir2018-full-report-english.pdf

40 OECD (2018), *OECD Employment Outlook 2018*, OECD Publishing, Paris, https://doi.org/10.1787/empl_outlook-2018-en

41 OECD (2019). Poverty rate (indicator). https://data.oecd.org/inequality/poverty-rate.htm

42 Stiglitz, J., Sen, A. and Fitoussi, J-P (2009). *Measuring Economic Performance and Social Progress*, Commission on the Measurement of Economic Performance and Social Progress. https://ec.europa.eu/eurostat/documents/118025/118123/Fitoussi+Commission+report. Boarini, R., Kolev, A. and McGregor, J.A. (2014). Measuring well-being and progress in countries at different stages of development: Towards a more universal conceptual framework. OECD Working Paper 325, OECD Publications. http://dx.doi.org/10.1787/5jxss4hv2d8n-en. Helliwell, J. F., Layard, R. and Sachs, J. (2012). *World Happiness Report 2012*. https://worldhappiness.report/ed/2012/

43 Stiglitz, J., Fitoussi, J. and Durand, M. (2018), Beyond GDP: *Measuring What Counts for Economic and Social Performance*, OECD Publishing. https://doi.org/10.1787/9789264307292-en. See also Case, A. and Deaton A. (2020), *Deaths of Despair and the Future of Capitalism*, Princeton University Press, 2020.

44 UNEP (2019), *Global Environment Outlook 6*. UN Environment Programme. https://www.unenvironment.org/resources/global-environment-outlook-6

45 OECD (2015). *In It Together: Why Less Inequality Benefits All*, OECD Publishing. http://dx.doi.org/10.1787/9789264235120-en. Berg A. and Ostry J. (2011) Inequality and sustainable growth: two sides of the same coin? International Monetary Fund. https://www.imf.org/en/Publications/Staff-Discussion-Notes/Issues/2016/12/31/Inequality-and-Unsustainable-Growth-Two-Sides-of-the-Same-Coin-24686. Cingano, F. (2014), Trends in Income Inequality and its Impact on Economic Growth, OECD Social, Employment and Migration Working Papers, No. 163, OECD Publishing. http://dx.doi.org/10.1787/5jxrjncwxv6j-en. Ostry J., Berg A. and Tsangarides C. (2014), Redistribution, inequality and growth, International Monetary Fund. https://www.imf.org/en/Publications/Staff-Discussion-Notes/Issues/2016/12/31/Redistribution-Inequality-and-Growth-41291

46 OECD (2015). *In It Together: Why Less Inequality Benefits All*, OECD Publishing. http://dx.doi.org/10.1787/9789264235120-en. Boushey, H. (2019). *Unbound: How Inequality Constricts Our Economy and What We Can Do About It*, Harvard University Press.

47 OECD (2018). *The Productivity-Inclusiveness Nexus*, OECD Publishing. https://doi.org/10.1787/9789264292932-en

48 Dabla-Norris, E. et al. (2015). Causes and consequences of income inequality: a global perspective. IMF Staff Discussion Notes No. 15/13. https://www.imf.org/en/Publications/Staff-Discussion-Notes/Issues/2016/12/31/Causes-and-Consequences-of-Income-Inequality-A-Global-Perspective-42986

49 Berg A. et al. (2018). Redistribution, inequality, and growth: new evidence. *Journal of Economic Growth*, 23 (6), 259-305

50 Boushey, H. (2019). *Unbound: How Inequality Constricts Our Economy and What We Can Do About It*. Harvard University Press. Case, A. and Deaton A. (2020), *Deaths of Despair and the Future of Capitalism*, Princeton University Press, 2020

51 Berg A. et al (2018). Redistribution, inequality, and growth: new evidence. *Journal of Economic Growth*, 23 (6), 259-305

52 Wilkinson, R. and Pickett, K. (2009) *The Spirit Level*. Allen Lane. Wilkinson, R. and Pickett, K. (2018). *The Inner Level*. Penguin

53 Helliwell, J. F., Layard, R., and Sachs, J. (2019). *World Happiness Report 2019*. https://worldhappiness.report/ed/2019/. Helliwell, J. F., Huang, H. and Wang, S. (2017). Chapter 2: The social foundations of world happiness. *World Happiness Report 2017*. https://worldhappiness.report/ed/2017/

54 World Bank (2012). *Inclusive Green Growth: The Pathway to Sustainable Development*. Washington, DC: World Bank. https://openknowledge.worldbank.org/handle/10986/6058. UNEP (2011). *Towards a Green Economy: Pathways to Sustainable Development and Poverty Eradication*. United Nations Environmental Programme. https://www.cbd.int/financial/doc/green_economyreport2011.pdf

55 Bowen, A. and Kuralbayeva, K. (2015). Looking for green jobs: the impact of green growth on employment. Grantham Research Institute on Climate Change and Environment and Global Green Growth Institute Policy Brief. http://www.lse.ac.uk/GranthamInstitute/wp-content/uploads/2015/03/Looking-for-green-jobs_the-impact-of-green-growth-on-employment.pdf

56 Business and Sustainable Development Commission (2017). *Better Business, Better World*. http://report.businesscommission.org/uploads/BetterBiz-BetterWorld_170215_012417.pdf. Webster, K. (2017). *The Circular Economy: A Wealth of Flows*, Ellen MacArthur Foundation, 2nd edn

57 Hickel, J. and Kallis, G. (2019). Is Green Growth Possible? *New Political Economy*, 1-18. https://doi.10.1080/13563467.2019.1598964. Institute for New Economic Thinking (2019). *Is Green Growth Possible: A Debate*. https://www.ineteconomics.org/perspectives/collections/is-green-growth-possible-a-debate

58 Jackson, T. (2016). *Prosperity Without Growth: Economics for a Finite Planet*. Routledge, 2nd edn.

59 McGregor, J.A. (2014) Poverty, wellbeing, and sustainability. In Neumayer, E, et al. (eds.), *The Handbook of Sustainable Development*, Edward Elgar.

60 OECD (2018), *Opportunities for All: A Framework for Policy Action on Inclusive Growth*, OECD Publishing, Paris, https://doi.org/10.1787/9789264301665-en. World Bank (2018). OECD (2011). *Towards Green Growth: A Summary for Policymakers*. OECD Publishing. https://www.oecd.org/greengrowth/48012345.pdf

61 https://www.un.org/sustainabledevelopment/sustainable-development-goals/

62 Hay, C., Hunt, T. and McGregor, J.A. (2019), Exploring the paradoxes of inclusive growth: towards a developmental, multilateral and multidimensional approach. Sheffield Political Economy Research Institute. http://speri.dept.shef.ac.uk/wp-content/uploads/2019/07/Exploring-the-paradoxes-of-inclusive-growth-towards-a-developmental-multilateral-and-multidimensional-approach-2.pdf

63 Stiglitz J., Sen, A. and Fitoussi, J-P. (2009), *Mismeasuring our Lives : Why GDP Doesn't Add Up*, The New Press. Coyle, D. (2014). *GDP: A Brief but Affectionate History*, Princeton University Press.

64 https://www.oecd.org/statistics/better-life-initiative.htm. https://www.oecd.org/inclusive-growth/

65 OECD Better Life Index (2019). http://www.oecdbetterlifeindex.org/. Stiglitz, J., Fitoussi, J. and Durand, M. (eds.) (2018), *For Good Measure: Advancing Research on Well-being Metrics Beyond GDP*, OECD Publishing. https://doi.org/10.1787/9789264307278-en

66 Alvaredo, F. et al. Distributional national accounts. In Stiglitz, J., Fitoussi, J. and Durand, M. (eds.) (2018), *For Good Measure: Advancing Research on Well-being Metrics Beyond GDP*, OECD Publishing, Paris, https://doi.org/10.1787/9789264307278-en

67 Government of New Zealand (2019). *The Wellbeing Budget 2019*. https://treasury.govt.nz/publications/wellbeing-budget/wellbeing-budget-2019-html. Scottish Government (2019). *National Performance Framework*. https://nationalperformance.gov.scot/

68 Hay, C., Hunt, T. and McGregor, J.A. (2019), Exploring the paradoxes of inclusive growth: towards a developmental, multilateral and multidimensional approach. Sheffield Political Economy Research Institute. http://speri.dept.shef.ac.uk/wp-content/uploads/2019/07/Exploring-the-paradoxes-of-inclusive-growth-towards-a-developmental-multilateral-and-multidimensional-approach-2.pdf

69 Bowles, S. and Carlin, W. (2020), What students learn in economics 101: time for a change, *Journal of Economic Literature* 58 (1), 176-214

70 Basu, L., Schifferes, S. and Knowles, S. (eds.) (2018), *The Media and Austerity: Comparative Perspectives*, Routledge

71 *Oxford Review of Economic Policy* (2018). Rebuilding Macroeconomic Theory. 34 (1-2)

72 Goodfriend, M. and King, R. G. (1997), The new neoclassical synthesis and the role of monetary policy, in Bernanke, B. and Rotemberg, J. (eds.) *NBER Macroeconomics Annual*. MIT Press, 231–82

73 Blyth, M. (2013). Paradigms and paradox: The politics of economic ideas in two moments of crisis. Governance, 26 (2), 197-215. Blyth, M., and Mark, B. (2002). *Great Transformations: Economic Ideas and Institutional Change in the Twentieth Century*. Cambridge University Press

74 Skidelsky, R. (2016), Economists versus the economy. *Project Syndicate*, 23 December. https://www.project-syndicate.org/commentary/mathematical-economics-training-too-narrow-by-robert-skidelsky-2016. *Guardian* (2017). 'Chief economist of Bank of England admits errors in Brexit forecasting', 5 January. https://www.theguardian.com/business/2017/jan/05/chief-economist-of-bank-of-england-admits-errors. Romer, P. (2016), The Trouble with Macroeconomics. Stern School of Business, New York University. https://economicsociologydotorg.files.wordpress.com/2018/10/the-trouble-with-macroeconomics-paul-romer.pdf. Rodrik, D. (2015). *Economics Rules: The Rights and Wrongs of the Dismal Science*. W. W. Norton & Co.

75 Wolf, M. (2014). *The Shifts and the Shocks: How the Financial Crisis Has Changed Our Future*. Penguin

76 See for example, Bank for International Settlements (2014), *84th Annual Report*. https://www.bis.org/publ/arpdf/ar2014e.pdf. Dagher, J. (2018), Regulatory cycles: revisiing the political economy of financial crises, IMF Working Paper WP/18/8. https://www.imf.org/en/Publications/WP/Issues/2018/01/15/Regulatory-Cycles-Revisiting-the-Political-Economy-of-Financial-Crises-45562

77 For a summary see for example Löfgren, K.-G., Persson, T. and Weibull, J. W. (2002), Markets with asymmetric information: the contributions of George Akerlof, Michael Spence and Joseph Stiglitz. *The Scandinavian Journal of Economics* 104 (2) 195-211

78 For a survey see for example *Oxford Review of Economic Policy* (2018). Rebuilding Macroeconomic Theory. 34 (1-2)

79 Bank for International Settlements (2018), *BIS Annual Economic Report 2018*. Chapter 4: Moving forward with macroprudential frameworks. https://www.bis.org/publ/arpdf/ar2018e4.htm

80 Rodrik, D. (2017). *Straight Talk on Trade: Ideas for a Sane World Economy*. Princeton University Press

81 OECD (2018). *A Broken Social Elevator? How to Promote Social Mobility*, OECD Publishing. https://doi.org/10.1787/9789264301085-en. Morel, N. and Palier, B. (eds.) (2011). *Towards a Social Investment Welfare State? Ideas, Policies and Challenges*. Policy Press. OECD (2017). *Report on the Implementation of the OECD Gender Recommendations*, OECD Publishing. http://www.oecd.org/mcm-2018/documents/C-MIN-2017-7-EN.pdf

82 See for example the work brought together by the Institute for New Economic Thinking. https://www.ineteconomics.org/

83 For useful surveys of 'heterodox' schools of economic thought, see Fischer, L. et al. (eds.) (2018). *Rethinking Economics: An Introduction to Pluralist Economics*, Routledge. Mearman, A., Berger, S. and Guizzo, D. (eds.) (2019). *What is Heterodox Economics?* Routledge

84 See for example Simon, H. A. (1955). A Behavioral Model of Rational Choice. *The Quarterly Journal of Economics* 69 (1), 99–118. Kahneman, D. (2011). *Thinking: Fast and Slow*. Allen Lane. Camerer, C., Loewenstein, G. and Rabin, M. (eds.) (2004). *Advances in Behavioral Economics*. Princeton University Press. Thaler, R. (2015). *Misbehaving: How Economics Became Behavioral*. Allen Lane. Thaler, R. and Sunstein, C. (2008). *Nudge: Improving Decisions About Health, Wealth and Happiness*. Penguin

85 See for example Ariely, D (2008), *Predictably Irrational: The Hidden Forces That Shape Our Decisions*. Harper Collins. Bowles, S. and Gintis, H. (2013). *A Cooperative Species: Human Reciprocity and Its Evolution*. Princeton University Press. Sandel, M. J. (2013). Market reasoning as moral reasoning: why economists should re-engage with political philosophy. *Journal of Economic Perspectives*, 27 (4), 121-40. Granovetter, J. (1997) *Society and Economy: The Social Construction of Economic Institutions*. Harvard University Press

86 McGregor, J.A. and Pouw, N. (2017). Towards an economics of wellbeing: what would economics look like if it were focused on human wellbeing?' *Cambridge Journal of Economics*, 41 (4), 1123–1142

87 Shiller, R. J. (2019). *Narrative Economics: How Stories Go Viral and Drive Major Economic Events*. Princeton University Press. Snower, D. J. and Akerlof, G. A. (2016), Bread and Bullet. Discussion Paper No. DP11132. https://papers.ssrn.com/sol3/papers.cfm?abstract_id=2766423##

88 See for example Furubotn, E. G. and Richter, R. (1997), *Institutions in Economic Theory: The Contribution of the New Institutional Economics*, University of Michigan Press. Hodgson, G. (2015). *Conceptualizing Capitalism: Institutions, Evolution, Future*. University of Chicago Press. Acemoglu, D. and Robinson, J. A. (2012). *Why Nations Fail: The Origins of Power, Prosperity, and Poverty*. Crown Business. North, D. C. (1990). *Institutions, Institutional Design and Economic Performance*. Cambridge University Press. Tirole, J. (1988). *The Theory of Industrial Organization*. MIT Press

89 Zuboff, S. (2019). *The Age of Surveillance Capitalism*. PublicAffairs / Profile Books. Srnicek, N. (2017). *Platform Capitalism*. Polity

90 See for example Hall, P.A. and Soskice D. (2001). *Varieties of Capitalism: The Institutional Foundations of Comparative Advantage*. Oxford University Press. Baccaro L. and Pontusson J. (2016). Rethinking comparative political economy, *Politics & Society*, 44(2), 175–207. Boyer, R. and Saillard, Y. (eds.) (2002), *Regulation Theory: The State of the Art*, Routledge

91 Bivens, J. and Shierholz, H. (2018). What labor market changes have generated inequality and wage suppression? Employment Policy Institute. https://www.epi.org/files/pdf/148880.pdf. Weil, D. (2017), *The Fissured Workplace*. Harvard University Press

92 Boushey, H. (2019). *Unbound: How Inequality Constricts Our Economy and What We Can Do About It*. Harvard University Press

93 Iversen, T. and Soskice, D. (2019). *Democracy and Prosperity: Reinventing Capitalism through a Turbulent Century*. Hay, C. and Payne. T. (2015), *Civic Capitalism*. Polity. Streeck, W. (2017). *How Will Capitalism End?* Verso

94 See for example Richard R. Nelson, R. R. and Winter, S. G. (1982). *An Evolutionary Theory of Economic Change*. Harvard University Press. Metcalfe, J. S. (1994). Evolutionary economics and technology policy. *The Economic Journal*, 104 (425), 931-944. Dopfer, K. and Potts, J. (2007). *The General Theory of Economic Evolution*. Routledge. Hodgson, G. A. (1993) *Economics and Evolution: Bringing Life Back Into Economics*, Cambridge University Press

95 Freeman, C. (2008). *Systems of Innovation: Selected Essays in Evolutionary Economics*. Edward Elgar Publishing. Perez, C. (2003). *Technological Revolutions and Financial Capital*, Edward Elgar Publishing

96 Mazzucato, M. (2013). *The Entrepreneurial State: Debunking Public vs Private Myths*. Anthem Press.

97 See for example Beinhocker, E. D. (2006). *The Origin of Wealth: Evolution, Complexity, and the Radical Remaking of Economics*. Harvard Business Press. Arthur, W. B. (2015). *Complexity and the Economy*. Oxford University Press. Wilson, D. S. and Kirman, A. (2016), *Complexity and Evolution: Toward a New Synthesis for Economics*. MIT Press. OECD, (2017) *Debate the Issues: Complexity and Policymaking*. OECD Insights. OECD Publishing. https://www.oecd.org/naec/complexity_and_policymaking.pdf

98 Hamill, L. and Gilbert, G. N. (2016). *Agent-based Modelling in Economics*. John Wiley & Sons

99 Wolf, M (2014). T*he Shifts and the Shocks: How the Financial Crisis Has Changed Our Future*. Penguin

100 Minsky, H. P. (1986). *Stabilizing an Unstable Economy*. Yale University Press. Minsky, H. P. (1992). The financial instability hypothesis. The Jerome Levy Economics Institute Working Paper, (74). http://www.levyinstitute.org/pubs/wp74.pdf

101 Lazonick. W. (2014) 'Profits without prosperity'. Harvard Business Review, September 2014. https://hbr.org/2014/09/profits-without-prosperity. Kay J. (2012). *The Kay Review of UK Equity Markets and Long-Term Decision Making*, HM Government http://www.ecgi.org/conferences/eu_actionplan2013/documents/kay_review_final_report.pdf. Nesvetailova, A. (2019). *Shadow Banking: Scope, Origins and Theories*, Routledge

102 See for example Carlin, W. and Soskice, D. (2006). *Macroeconomics: Imperfections, Institutions and Policies*, Oxford University Press. Lavoie, M. (2014). *Post-Keynesian Economics: New Foundations*, Edward Elgar. King, J. (2003). *The Elgar Companion to Post-Keynesian Economics*. Edward Elgar

103 Summers L. (2016) The age of secular stagnation: what it is and what to do about it. *Foreign Affairs* 95 (2)

104 Blanchard, O (2019), Public Debt and Low Interest Rates. *American Economic Review* 109 (4), 1197-1229

105 Griffith-Jones S. and Cozzi G. (2016) 'Investment-led growth: a solution to the European crisis', in Jacobs M. and Mazzucato M. (eds) *Rethinking Capitalism: Economics and Policy for Sustainable and Inclusive Growth*, Wiley Blackwell.

106 McLeay, M., Radia, A. and Thomas, R. (2014). Money creation in the modern economy. *Bank of England Quarterly Bulletin*. https://www.bankofengland.co.uk/-/media/boe/files/quarterly-bulletin/2014/money-creation-in-the-modern-economy.pdf

107 See for example Wray, L. R. (2015), *Modern Money Theory: A Primer on Macroeconomics for Sovereign Monetary Systems*, Springer

108 Stiglitz, J. (2018). Where modern macroeconomics went wrong, *Oxford Review of Economic Policy* 34 (1-2), 70-106. Wren-Lewis, S. (2018). Ending the microfoundations hegemony. *Oxford Review of Economic Policy*, 34 (1-2), 55-69

109 Hendry, D. and Muellbauer, J (2018). The future of macroeconomics: macro theory and models at the Bank of England. *Oxford Review of Economic Policy*, 34 (1-2), 287-328. Muellbauer, J. (2018). The future of macroeconomics. INET Oxford Working Paper No 2018-10. https://www.inet.ox.ac.uk/files/5-June-18_John_Muellbauer-_The_Future_of_Macroeconomics_rev_Nov_10.pdf

110 See for example Tietenberg, T and Lewis, L (2018), *Environmental and Natural Resource Economics, Routledge*, 11th edn

111 See for example Georgescu-Roegen, N. (1971). *The Entropy Law and the Economic Process*, Harvard University Press. Martinez-Alier, J. Ecological Economics: Energy, Environment and Society, Blackwell. Daly, H. and Farley, J. (2003), *Ecological Economics: Principles and Applications*, Island Press. Spash, C. L. (ed) (2017). *Routledge Handbook of Ecological Economics*. Routledge

112 Steffen, W. et al. (2015). Planetary boundaries: Guiding human development on a changing planet. *Science*, 347 (6223), 1259855-1-10. https://science.sciencemag.org/content/sci/347/6223/1259855.full.pdf

113 Grubb, M (2014), *Planetary Economics: Energy, Climate Change and the Three Domains of Sustainable Development*, Routledge

114 Victor P. (2019). *Managing Without Growth: Slower by Design, Not Disaster*. Edward Elgar, 2nd edn. Jackson, T. (2018). The post-growth challenge: secular stagnation, inequality and the limits to growth, CUSP Working Paper, https://timjackson.org.uk/the-post-growth-challenge/. Hickel, J. and Kallis, G. (2019). Is Green Growth Possible? *New Political Economy*, 1-18. https://doi.10.1080/13563467.2019.1598964. Institute for New Economic Thinking (2019). *Is Green Growth Possible: A Debate*. https://www.ineteconomics.org/perspectives/collections/is-green-growth-possible-a-debate

115 See for example Piketty, T. (2013). *Capital in the Twenty-First Century*. Harvard University Press, Atkinson. A. B. (2015). *Inequality: What Can Be Done?* Harvard University Press. Milanovic, B. (2018). *Global Inequality: A New Approach for the Age of Globalization*. Belknap Press. Piketty, T. and Zucman, G. (2014). Capital is back: wealth–income ratios in rich countries, 1700–2010, *The Quarterly Journal of Economics* 129 (3): 1255–310. Atkinson, A. B., Piketty, T. and Saez, E. (2011). Top incomes in the long run of history. *Journal of Economic Literature*, 49 (1), 3-71. Stiglitz, J. (2012) *The Price of Inequality*, Penguin. Bowles, S. (2013). *The New Economics of Inequality and Redistribution*. Cambridge University Press. Chetty, R. et al. (2016). The fading American dream: trends in absolute income mobility since 1940. NBER Working Paper 22910. http://www.equality-of-opportunity.org/papers/abs_mobility_paper.pdf

116 Rodrik, D. (2017). *Straight Talk on Trade: Ideas for a Sane World Economy*. Princeton University Press

117 Chang, H.-J. (2010). *Bad Samaritans: The Myth of Free Trade and the Secret History of Capitalism*. Bloomsbury

118 OECD (2018). *OECD Employment Outlook 2018*, OECD Publishing. https://doi.org/10.1787/empl_outlook-2018-en

119 Piketty, T. (2013). *Capital in the Twenty-First Century*. Harvard University Press. Stiglitz, J. (2016). Inequality and economic growth. In Jacobs, M. and Mazzucato, M. (eds.) *Rethinking Capitalism: Economics and Policy for Sustainable and Inclusive Growth*. Wiley Blackwell. Standing, G. (2016). *The Corruption of Capitalism: Why Rentiers Thrive and Work Does Not Pay*. Biteback

120 Farber, H. S. et al. (2018). Unions and inequality over the twentieth century: new evidence from survey data. NBER Working Paper No 24587. https://www.nber.org/papers/w24587. Bivens, J. and Shierholz, H. (2018). What labor market changes have generated inequality and wage suppression? Employment Policy Institute. https://www.epi.org/files/pdf/148880.pdf. Bahn, K. (2019) 'Skills gap' arguments overlook collective bargaining and low minimum wages. Washington Centre for Equitable Growth. https://equitablegrowth.org/skills-gap-arguments-overlook-collective-bargaining-and-low-minimum-wages/

121 Stiglitz, J. (2012) *The Price of Inequality*, Penguin. Boushey, H. (2019). *Unbound: How Inequality Constricts Our Economy and What We Can Do About It*. Harvard University Press. Wilkinson, R. and Pickett, K. (2009) *The Spirit Level*. Allen Lane. Wilkinson, R. and Pickett, K. (2018). *The Inner Level*. Penguin Books

122 OECD (2019), Gender wage gap (indicator). https://doi: 10.1787/7cee77aa-en (accessed on 5 July 2019). OECD (2019). *Social Institutions and Gender Index* (SIGI) Annual Report. OECD Publishing. https://www.oecd-ilibrary.org/development/sigi-2019-global-report_bc56d212-en

123 See for example Blau, F. D., Ferber, M. A. and Winkler, A. E. (2014). *The Economics of Women, Men and Work*. Pearson, 7th edition. Goldin, C. (2014). A grand gender convergence: its last chapter. *American Economic Review* 104 (4), 1091–1119. https://scholar.harvard.edu/files/goldin/files/goldin_aeapress_2014_1.pdf

124 See for example Waring, M. (1988). *If Women Counted: A New Feminist Economics*. Harper & Row. Ferber, M. A. and Nelson, J. A. (eds.) (1993). *Beyond Economic Man: Feminist Theory and Economics*. University of Chicago Press. Nelson, J. A. (1995). Feminism and economics. *The Journal of Economic Perspectives* 9 (2), 131-148. Power, M. (2004). Social provisioning as a starting point for feminist economics. *Feminist Economics* 10 (3), 3-19. Kuiper, E. & Sap, J. (eds.) (1995), *Out of the Margin: Feminist Perspectives on Economics*. Routledge

125 OECD (2008). *OECD Employment Outlook 2008*. Chapter 3: The price of prejudice: labour market discrimination on the grounds of gender and ethnicity. OECD Publishing. Akee, R., Jones, M. R. and Porter, S. R. (2017). Race matters: income shares, income inequality, and income mobility for all U.S. races. NBER Working Paper No. 23733. Acemoglu, D, Johnson, S. and Robinson, J. A. (2001) The colonial origins of comparative development: an empirical investigation. *American Economic Review*, 91, 1369-1401. Collins, P. H. and Bilge, S. (2016). *Intersectionality*. Wiley

126 Folbre, N. (2008). *Valuing children: rethinking the economics of the family*. Harvard University Press. Folbre, N. and Bittman, M. (2004). *Family Time: The Social Organization of Care*. Routledge. Himmelweit, S. (2002), Making visible the hidden economy: the case for gender-impact analysis of economic policy. *Feminist Economics*, 8 (1), 49-70

127 Wight, J. B. (2015), *Ethics in Economics: An Introduction to Moral Frameworks*, Stanford University Press

128 Nolt, J (2017). Future generations in environmental ethics, in Gardiner, S and Thompson, A. (eds.) *The Oxford Handbook of Environmental Ethics*, Oxford University Press

129 Sandel, M. J. (2013). Market reasoning as moral reasoning: why economists should re-engage with political philosophy. *Journal of Economic Perspectives*, 27 (4), 121-40. Sandel, M. J. (2012). *What Money Can't Buy: The Moral Limits of Markets*. Farrar, Straus and Giroux. Bowles, S. (2016). *The Moral Economy*. Yale University Press. Komlos, J. (2019). *Foundations of Real-World Economics*. Routledge, 2nd edn

130 Mazzucato M. (2016). From market fixing to market-creating: a new framework for innovation policy". *Industry and Innovation*, 23 (2), 140-156. Kattel, R. et al. (2018). The economics of change: policy appraisal for missions, market shaping and public purpose. UCL Institute for Innovation and Public Purpose Working Paper. https://www.ucl.ac.uk/bartlett/public-purpose/publications/2018/jul/economics-change-policy-and-appraisal-missions-market-shaping-and-public. Hay, C. and Payne, T. (2015), *Civic Capitalism*. Polity

131 Mearman, A., Berger, S. and Guizzo, D. (eds.) (2019). *What is Heterodox Economics?* Routledge

Coyle, D. (2007), *The Soulful Science: What Economists Really Do and Why it Matters*. Princeton University Press. Fischer, L. et al. (2018). *Rethinking Economics: An Introduction to Pluralist Economics*, Routledge. See also the work brought together by the Institute for New Economic Thinking. https://www.ineteconomics.org/

132 https://www.nobelprize.org/prizes/lists/all-prizes-in-economic-sciences/

133 Fox, J. (2016). How economics went from theory to data. *Bloomberg Opinion*. https://www.bloomberg.com/opinion/articles/2016-01-06/how-economics-went-from-theory-to-data. Hamermesh, D. S. (2013). Six decades of top economics publishing: who and how? *Journal of Economic Literature*, 51 (1), 162-72

134 Zucman, G., Rodrik, D. and Naidu, S. (2019). Economics after neoliberalism. *Boston Review*, 15 February. http://bostonreview.net/forum/suresh-naidu-dani-rodrik-gabriel-zucman-economics-after-neoliberalism. Rodrik, D. (2015). *Economics Rules: The Rights and Wrongs of the Dismal Science*. W. W. Norton & Co. Colander, C., Holt, R. and Rosser, B. (2004). The changing face of mainstream economics. *Review of Political Economy* 16 (4), 485-499

135 Beinhocker. E. et al. (2019). Forum response: economics after neoliberalism. *Boston Review*, 19 March. Kvangraven, I. and Alves, C. (2019). Heterodox economics as a positive project: revisiting the debate. ESRC GPID Research Network Working Paper 19. https://www.gpidnetwork.org/wp-content/uploads/2019/07/GPID-WP-19.pdf

136 Bowles, S. and Carlin, W. (2020), What students learn in economics 101: time for a change, *Journal of Economic Literature* 58 (1), 176-214. See also https://www.core-econ.org/

137 Wilson, D. S. and Kirman, A. (2016), *Complexity and Evolution: Toward a New Synthesis for Economics*. MIT Press

138 See for example the journals *New Political Economy* https://www.tandfonline.com/loi/cnpe20 and the *Review of International Political Economy* https://www.tandfonline.com/loi/rrip20

139 For collections of policy ideas (in English), see for example IPPR Commission on Economic Justice (2018). *Prosperity and Justice: A Plan for the New Economy*. Institute for Public Policy Research / Polity. https://www.ippr.org/research/publications/prosperity-and-justice. Economics for Inclusive Prosperity. https://econfip.org. Stiglitz, J. et al. (2019). *Rewriting the Rules of the European Economy*. Foundation for European Progressive Studies.

https://www.feps-europe.eu/attachments/publications/book_stiglitz-web-pp.pdf. Abernathy, N., Hamilton, D. and Morgan, J. M. (2019). *New Rules for the 21st Century: Corporate Power, Public Power, and the Future of the American Economy.* Roosevelt Institute

140 Tett, G. (2015). *The Silo Effect.* Little, Brown

141 Jacobs, M. (2018). Only revolutionary new laws can stop Brexit harming the environment. *Guardian*, 3 April. https://www.theguardian.com/commentisfree/2018/apr/03/brexit-harm-environment-michael-gove

142 OECD (2017). *Investing in Climate, Investing in Growth*, OECD Publishing. https://doi.org/10.1787/9789264273528-en. Global Commission on the Economy and Climate (2014). *Better Growth Better Climate: The New Climate Economy Report.* https://newclimateeconomy.report/2014/misc/downloads/. Business and Sustainable Development Commission (2017). *Better Business, Better World.* http://report.businesscommission.org/uploads/BetterBiz-BetterWorld_170215_012417.pdf

143 Coady, D. et al. (2019). Global fossil fuel subsidies remain large: an update based on country-level estimates. IMF Working Paper 19/89. https://www.imf.org/en/Publications/WP/Issues/2019/05/02/Global-Fossil-Fuel-Subsidies-Remain-Large-An-Update-Based-on-Country-Level-Estimates-46509

144 ITUC Just Transition Centre (2018). *Just Transition: A Business Guide.* International Trade Union Confederation / The B Team. https://www.ituc-csi.org/IMG/pdf/just_transition_-_a_business_guide.pdf. ILO (2018). Just transition towards environmentally sustainable economies and societies for all. ILO / ACTRAV Policy Brief. International Labour Organization. hhttps://www.ilo.org/actrav/info/pubs/WCMS_647648/lang--en/index.htm

145 Mazzucato, M. (2017). 'Mission-oriented innovation policy: challenges and opportunities'. UCL Institute for Innovation and Public Purpose Working Paper 17-01. https://www.ucl.ac.uk/bartlett/publicpurpose/sites/public-purpose/files/moip-challengesand-opportunities-working-paper-2017-1.pdf. Mazzucato, M. (2018). *Mission-Oriented Research & Innovation in the EU: A Problem-solving Approach to Fuel Innovation-led Growth.* https://publications.europa.eu/da/publication-detail/-/publication/5b2811d1-16be-11e8-9253-01aa75ed71a1/language-en

146 Democracy Collaborative (2014). *Policies for Community Wealth Building: Leveraging State and Local Resources.* https://democracycollaborative.org/cwbpolicy

147 Boone, L (2019). Global growth is weakening: coordinating on fiscal and structural policies can revive euro area growth. OECD Ecoscope. https://oecdecoscope.blog/2019/03/06/global-growth-is-weakening-coordinating-on-fiscal-and-structural-policies-can-revive-euro-area-growth/

148 Blanchard, O (2019), Public debt and low interest rates. *American Economic Review* 109 (4), 1197-1229

149 Buiter, W. (2018). The financial system ten years after the financial crisis: lessons learnt. Presentation to OECD NAEC conference. http://www.oecd.org/naec/10-years-after-the-crisis/W_Buiter_NAEC_14_Sept_2018.pdf. Tucker, P. (2019). Is the financial system sufficiently resilient: a research programme and policy agenda. Bank for International Settlements Working Paper No 792. https://www.bis.org/publ/work792.pdf

150 Aikman, D. et al. (2018). Would macroprudential regulation have prevented the last crisis? Bank of England Staff Working Paper No. 747. https://www.bankofengland.co.uk/-/media/boe/files/working-paper/2018/would-macroprudential-regulation-have-prevented-the-last-crisis.pdf. Lysandrou, P. and Nesvetailova, A. (2015). The role of shadow banking entities in the financial crisis: a disaggregated view. *Review of International Political Economy*, 22 (2), 257-279

151 Baker, A., Epstein, G. and Montecino, J. (2019). The UK's finance curse? Costs and processes. Sheffield Political Economy Research Institute. https://speri.dept.shef.ac.uk/wp-content/uploads/2019/01/SPERI-The-UKs-Finance-Curse-Costs-and-Processes.pdf

152 See for example Mian, A. (2019). How to think about finance. In Naidu, S., Rodrik, D. and Zucman, G. (eds.) *Economics for Inclusive Prosperity: An Introduction.* https://econfip.org/wp-content/uploads/2019/02/Economics-for-Inclusive-Prosperity.pdf. Stirling, A. and King, L. (2017) Financing Investment: Reforming Finance Markets for the Long-Term, IPPR. https://www.ippr.org/publications/cej-financing-investment. Admati, A. R. (2019). Towards a better financial system. In Naidu, S., Rodrik, D. and Zucman, G. (eds.) *Economics for Inclusive Prosperity: An Introduction.* https://econfip.org/wp-content/uploads/2019/02/Economics-for-Inclusive-Prosperity.pdf. Van Lerven, F. (2018). The Bank of England and a 1.5C Transition: Reshaping Finance. New Economics Foundation Briefing Paper. https://neweconomics.org/uploads/files/reshaping-finance.pdf. Burman, L. E. et al. (2015). Financial transaction taxes in theory and practice. Tax Policy Center. https://www.taxpolicycenter.org/publications/financial-transaction-taxes-theory-and-practice

153 Lazonick, W. and O'Sullivan, M. (2000). Maximizing shareholder value: a new ideology for corporate governance. *Economy and Society*, 29 (1), 13-35. Lawrence, M. (2017). *Corporate Governance Reform: Turning Business Towards Long-term Success*, Institute for Public Policy Research. https://www.ippr.org/files/2017-07/cej-cgr-dp-17-07-14.pdf

154 Khan, L. M. (2016). Amazon's antitrust paradox. *Yale Law Journal*, 126 (3), 710-805. Lynn, B. C. (2017). The consumer welfare standard in antitrust: outdated or a harbor in a sea of doubt? Open Markets Institute. https://www.judiciary.senate.gov/imo/media/doc/12-13-17%20Lynn%20Testimony.pdf

155 See for example Zuboff, S. (2019). *The Age of Surveillance Capitalism*. PublicAffairs / Profile Books. Lawrence, M. and Laybourn-Langton, L. (2018). *The digital commonwealth: from private enclosure to collective benefit*. Institute for Public Policy Research. https://www.ippr.org/research/publications/the-digital-commonwealth.Feld, Feld, H. (2019). *The Case For The Digital Platform Act: Market Structure And Regulation Of Digital Platforms*. Roosevelt Institute / Public Knowledge. https://www.publicknowledge.org/assets/uploads/documents/Case_for_the_Digital_Platform_Act_Harold_Feld_2019.pdf

156 See for example Applebaum, R. and Lichtenstein, N. (eds.) (2016). *Achieving Workers' Rights in the Global Economy*. Cornell University Press. Bartley, T. (2018). *Rules without Rights: Land, Labor and Private Authority in the Global Economy*. Oxford University Press

157 See for example Rodrik, D. (2019). Towards a more inclusive globalization: an anti-social dumping scheme. In Naidu, S., Rodrik, D. and Zucman, G. (eds.) *Economics for Inclusive Prosperity: An Introduction*. https://econfip.org/wp-content/uploads/2019/02/Economics-for-Inclusive-Prosperity.pdf

158 See for example Zucman, G. (2019). Taxing multinational corporations in the 21st century. In Naidu, S., Rodrik, D. and Zucman, G. (eds.) *Economics for Inclusive Prosperity: An Introduction*. https://econfip.org/wp-content/uploads/2019/02/Economics-for-Inclusive-Prosperity.pdf. Picciotto, S. (2012). Towards unitary taxation of transnational corporations. Tax Justice Network. https://www.taxjustice.net/wp-content/uploads/2013/04/Towards-Unitary-Taxation-Picciotto-2012.pdf. OECD (2015). *Addressing the Tax Challenges of the Digital Economy, Action 1 - 2015 Final Report*, OECD/G20 Base Erosion and Profit Shifting Project. OECD Publishing. https://www.oecd-ilibrary.org/taxation/addressing-the-tax-challenges-of-the-digital-economy-action-1-2015-final-report_9789264241046-en

159 Boushey, H. (2019). *Unbound: How Inequality Constricts Our Economy and What We Can Do About It*. Harvard University Press. Lustig, N (ed.) (2018). *Commitment to Equity Handbook: Estimating the Impact of Fiscal Policy on Inequality and Poverty*. Brookings Institution Press and CEQ Institute, Tulane University. https://www.dropbox.com/s/525sxekfco4vs4m/1.%20CEQ%20Handbook_2018%20-%20Lustig%20%28Editor%29.pdf?dl=0

160 Alvaredo, F. et al. (eds.). (2018). *World Inequality Report 2018*. Belknap Press. https://wir2018.wid.world/files/download/wir2018-full-report-english.pdf

161 See for example Gowan, P. and Lawrence, M. (2019). Democratic ownership funds: creating shared wealth and power. Next System Project / Common Wealth. https://common-wealth.co.uk/Democratic-ownership-funds-creating-shared-wealth-and-power.html. Ryan-Collins, J., Lloyd, T. and Macfarlane, L (2017). *Rethinking the Economics of Land and Housing*. Zed Books. Roberts, C and Lawrence, M (2018), *Our Common Wealth: A Citizens Wealth Fund for the UK*. Institute for Public Policy Research. https://www.ippr.org/research/publications/our-common-wealth

162 See for example IPPR Commission on Economic Justice (2018). *Prosperity and Justice: A Plan for the New Economy*, Institute for Public Policy Research / Polity. Saez, E. and Zucman, G. (2019). *How would a progressive wealth tax work? Evidence from the economic literature*. University of California, Berkeley. http://gabriel-zucman.eu/files/saez-zucman-wealthtaxobjections.pdf

163 See for example Boushey, H. (2019). *Unbound: How Inequality Constricts Our Economy and What We Can Do About It*. Harvard University Press. Naidu, S. (2019). Worker collective action in the 21th Century labor market. In Naidu, S., Rodrik, D. and Zucman, G. (eds.) *Economics for Inclusive Prosperity: An Introduction*. https://econfip.org/wp-content/uploads/2019/02/Economics-for-Inclusive-Prosperity.pdf. Dube, A. (2019). Using wage boards to raise pay. In Naidu, S., Rodrik, D. and Zucman, G. (eds.) *Economics for Inclusive Prosperity: An Introduction*. https://econfip.org/wp-content/uploads/2019/02/Economics-for-Inclusive-Prosperity.pdf

164 See for example Korinek, A. (2019). Labor in the age of automation and artificial intelligence. In Naidu, S., Rodrik, D. and Zucman, G. (eds.) *Economics for Inclusive Prosperity: An Introduction*. https://econfip.org/wp-content/uploads/2019/02/Economics-for-Inclusive-Prosperity.pdf

165 Tcherneva, P (2018), The job guarantee: design, jobs and implementation, Levy Economics Institute Working Paper No 902. http://www.levyinstitute.org/pubs/wp_902.pdf

166 Wilthagen, T. and Tros, F. (2004). The concept of 'flexicurity': a new approach to regulating employment and labour markets. *Transfer: European Review of Labour and Research*, 10 (2), 166-186. Andersen, T. M. and Svarer, M. (2007). Flexicurity—labour market performance in Denmark. *CESifo Economic Studie*s, 53 (3), 389-429

167 Standing, G. (2017). *Basic Income: And How We Can Make it Happen*. Pelican. Van Parijs, P. and Vanderborght, Y. (2017). *Basic Income: A Radical Proposal for a Free Society and a Sane Economy*. Harvard University Press

168 Social Prosperity Network (2017). Social prosperity for the future: A proposal for Universal Basic Services. UCL Institute for Global Prosperity. https://www.ucl.ac.uk/bartlett/igp/sites/bartlett/files/universal_basic_services_-_the_institute_for_global_prosperity_.pdf. Gough, I. (2019). Universal basic services: a theoretical and moral framework. *The Political Quarterly*. June. https://onlinelibrary.wiley.com/doi/abs/10.1111/1467-923X.12706

169 See for example Boushey, H. (2019). *Unbound: How Inequality Constricts Our Economy and What We Can Do About It*. Harvard University Press

170 See for example Coote, A. and Franklin, J. (eds.) (2013). *Time on our Side: Why We All Need a Shorter Working Week*. New Economics Foundation. https://neweconomics.org/campaigns/shorter-working-week

171 Hay, C., Hunt, T. and McGregor, J.A. (2019), Exploring the paradoxes of inclusive growth: towards a developmental, multilateral and multidimensional approach. Sheffield Political Economy Research Institute. http://speri.dept.shef.ac.uk/wp-content/uploads/2019/07/Exploring-the-paradoxes-of-inclusive-growth-towards-a-developmental-multilateral-and-multidimensional-approach-2.pdf

172 See for example Tam, H. (ed.) (2019). *Whose Government Is It? The Renewal of State-Citizen Cooperation*. Bristol University Press. Smith, G. (2009). *Democratic Innovations: Designing Institutions for Citizen Participation*. Cambridge University Press. Fishkin, J. S. (2011). *When the People Speak: Deliberative Democracy and Public Consultation*. Oxford University Press. See also https://citizensassembly.co.uk/

173 See for example OECD. (2017). *New Approaches to Economic Challenges: Towards a New Narrative*. Chapter 4: Towards an empowering state. OECD Publishing. Cottam, H. (2018). *Radical Help: How We Can Remake the Relationships Between Us and Revolutionise the Welfare State*. Virago

174 Snower, D. (2019). A new societal contract. *Economics*: 13 (2019-37), 1-13. http://dx.doi.org/10.5018/economics-ejournal.ja.2019-37. Mazzucato, M. (2013). *The Entrepreneurial State*. Anthem Press. Hay, C. and Payne. T. (2015), *Civic Capitalism*. Polity

175 Laybourn-Langton, L. and Jacobs, M. (2018). Paradigm shifts in economic theory and policy. *Intereconomics: Review of European Economic Policy*, 53 (3), 113-118. https://archive.intereconomics.eu/year/2018/3/paradigm-shifts-in-economic-theory-and-policy/

176 Ibid.